COMPLETING THE HUNT

COOKING GAME WITH NAHC MEMBERS

Minnetonka, Minnesota

COMPLETING THE HUNT
COOKING GAME WITH NAHC MEMBERS

Printed in 2012.

Tom Carpenter
Creative Director

Julie Cisler, Shari Gross
Book Design and Production

Heather Koshiol
Book Development Coordinator

Laura Holle
Book Development Assistant

Lee Kline
Photo, pages 2–3

Phil Aarrestad Photography
Food Photography

Cindy Ojczyk
Food Stylist

Betsy Nelson
Food Stylist

Martha Hall Foose
Assistant Stylist

Pegi Lee
Assistant Stylist

John Keenen
Assistant Photographer

Juli Hansen
Prop Stylist

Special thanks to: Red Cedar Deer Ranch

ISBN 10: 1-58159-158-6
ISBN 13: 978-1-58159-158-3

9 10 / 15 14 13 12

© 2002 North American Hunting Club

North American Hunting Club
12301 Whitewater Drive
Minnetonka, MN 55343
www.huntingclub.com

TABLE OF CONTENTS

INTRODUCTION

I like to extend my deer hunting seasons, usually until about next spring's turkey hunts. If the turkey chasing is good, I might finish that hunt around the fourth of July. Somewhere in there, I'll put the finishing touches on any bird hunting I managed to cram in.

But the local game warden doesn't seem to mind these hunting season extensions. That's because it's the cooking and eating of the game that's taking place!

For some, the hunt ends upon pulling the trigger or releasing an arrow. The meat is eaten and appreciated, of course, but the excitement is over when the game is in hand.

Others consider the hunt "on" until the game is field dressed, transported home and in the freezer or smoker. The work—which may include skinning and cutting up a deer—is an essential and enjoyable part of the hunt, but that's that.

But there is another reality. Eating game is a necessary and fun part of completing the hunt … as essential as scouting, sighting in, being in the field, making the shot, everything.

That's what *Completing the Hunt: Cooking Game with NAHC Members* is all about. Here are more than 250 wonderful recipes, direct from NAHC members, for creating awesome game meals. These cooking ideas, proven in member kitchens across North America, will do your game proud. You'll look to this book as a natural part of every hunt.

When I'm throwing a venison chop on the grill, I'm back in my treestand the morning the buck ghosted through the oaks and hazelbrush as the sun cracked the horizon.

When I'm roasting a turkey breast, I'm on a West Virginia mountainside again, the redbud in bloom around, feeling my heart beat for real as the jake sneaked in.

When I'm eating baked squirrel in my Mom's kitchen, I'm a twelve-year stalking through the oak woodlots of my youth again.

When I'm sauteing a pair of ruffed grouse breasts, my heart whirs faster at the thought of the magnificent bird topping out against a bank of golden popple trees and then tumbling to the ground with a pleasing "thump" at the sound of my shot.

It's time to extend your hunting seasons, celebrate the chase and commemorate the game as you complete your hunts in delicious style.

Tom

Tom Carpenter

Chapter 1

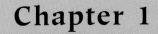

VENISON
Steaks, Chops, Roasts & More

Any deer will provide many meals' worth of great eating. Shoot an extra-big buck, or bring home a couple animals over the course of the season, and you've got an extra blessing of game meat to enjoy. Make the most of the prime cuts—and don't get bored with the fantastic taste of good venison—by using these premier recipes.

VENISON WITH SNOW PEAS
IN OYSTER SAUCE

1 lb. venison, sliced across the grain, ⅛ x
    1 x 2 inches

MARINADE
1 tsp. minced ginger
1 T. minced garlic
3 T. chopped green onion
2 T. sesame oil

SAUCE
2 cups chicken broth
1 T. cornstarch
1 large diced red pepper
½ lb. snow peas
1 cup oyster sauce

Prepare marinade: Mix ginger, garlic, green onion and oil. Add meat and marinate for 1 to 2 hours in refrigerator.

In separate bowl, mix chicken broth and cornstarch; set aside. Heat wok or sauté pan. Add meat, brown and remove. Stir-fry red peppers and snow peas. Add cornstarch mixture and oyster sauce to wok. Heat to boiling and cook until thick. Return meat to pan; blend and serve over rice or noodles.

Edward Sibole
Gerrardstown, West Virginia

BAVARIAN VENISON

1½ lbs. venison loin or steak, cut into 2-inch pieces
¼ cup flour
Pinch of cayenne pepper
2 T. olive oil
Salt
Pepper
10.5-oz. can consommé
¾ cup red cooking wine
1 medium onion, sliced
1 slice bread, cut into ½-inch cubes

Mix flour and cayenne pepper. Coat meat and brown in olive oil in large skillet. Add salt, pepper, consommé, wine, onion and bread. Mix well. Cover and cook over low heat for 1 hour, stirring occasionally. Serve over mashed potatoes with hot buttered rolls.

Jammy Place
Kentwood, Michigan

STUFFED VENISON ROAST

3 to 4 lbs. boneless deer, antelope, elk or moose roast, up to 1 inch thick
6 slices bacon
1 medium onion, chopped
½ cup chopped celery
½ cup chopped carrot
⅓ cup seasoned bread crumbs
2 tsp. dried parsley flakes
¼ tsp. salt
⅛ tsp. pepper
3 slices bacon, cut in half

Fry 6 slices of bacon in large skillet over medium heat until crisp. Remove from heat and transfer to paper towel to drain excess grease. Reserve 3 tablespoons bacon fat. Crumble dried bacon and set aside. Cook and stir onion, celery and carrots in reserved bacon fat over medium heat until tender. Remove from heat and stir in crumbled bacon, bread crumbs, parsley, salt and pepper.

Spread vegetable mixture evenly on roast. Pat firmly into place. Roll up jelly-roll-style, rolling with grain of meat. Tie roast with kitchen string. Place in roasting pan and top with 3 halved slices of bacon. Roast at 350°F to 375°F to desired doneness or about 22 to 30 minutes per pound.

Note: If using moose or elk, roast may need to be cut in half and half frozen for another time.

Vince Stracke
TyTy, Georgia

VENISON JAMBALAYA

1 lb. venison loin or cube steak
Salt
Pepper
Extra virgin olive oil
4 cups cooked long-grain rice
½ cup diced onion
¼ cup diced green bell pepper
¼ tsp. salt
¼ tsp. paprika
¼ cup minced garlic
¼ cup soy sauce
¼ tsp. ground red pepper
½ lb. cooked cocktail shrimp, diced

Season venison with salt and pepper; sauté in olive oil for 15 minutes over medium-high heat. Reduce heat to medium-low and simmer, covered, for 1 hour, stirring occasionally. Add rice, onion, green bell pepper, salt, paprika, garlic, soy sauce, red pepper and shrimp. Cook on medium for 25 minutes.

Jeff Middendorf
Lawrenceburg, Indiana

Herbed Venison Tenderloin
with Béarnaise Sauce

3 lbs. fresh venison tenderloin or backstrap
½ cup olive oil
1 T. balsamic vinegar or sherry
¼ cup fresh or ⅛ cup dried parsley
1 tsp. fresh or ½ tsp. dried thyme
1 bay leaf
2 cloves garlic, crushed

Béarnaise Sauce

1 T. minced shallot
2 tsp. minced fresh or ½ tsp. dried tarragon
Salt
Pepper
½ cup white wine
2 egg yolks
1 T. water
½ cup (1 stick) butter
Lemon juice (optional)
Garlic (optional)

Combine olive oil, vinegar or sherry, parsley, thyme, bay leaf and garlic; add meat and marinate for 1 hour. Remove meat from marinade and pat dry. Roast meat for 20 to 30 minutes at 450°F or until thickest part of meat reaches desired doneness (140°F for medium). Let meat cool slightly, then cut into thick slices. Serve with Béarnaise Sauce (below).

In small saucepan, combine shallot, tarragon, salt, pepper and wine. Cook over low heat until all but 2 tablespoons of wine has evaporated. Beat egg yolks with water and stir into saucepan. Cook over low heat, stirring continuously with wire whisk until sauce is thick. With heat as low as possible, add butter a bit at a time. Add a bit of lemon juice or garlic, if desired. Season with more salt and pepper. If sauce becomes too thick, stir in a bit more water. Serve immediately.

Terry Mann
Mosinee, Wisconsin

John's Venison Hunter's Stew

2 lbs. venison, cut into cubes
1½ cups flour
½ tsp. salt
½ tsp. pepper
1 tsp. garlic powder
1 tsp. onion powder
1 tsp. paprika
Oil
5 cloves garlic
3 (14½-oz.) cans beef broth
5 carrots, sliced
5 large potatoes, cubed
3 celery ribs, sliced
14½-oz. can tomato sauce
4 fresh plum tomatoes or 2 medium tomatoes, diced
1 large onion, sliced
3 T. soy sauce
1 T. Worcestershire sauce
½ tsp. rosemary
½ tsp. thyme
½ tsp. sage
Dash of cayenne pepper

Mix flour, salt, pepper, garlic powder, onion powder and paprika. Coat meat with flour mixture and brown in hot oil. Heat oil in separate soup pot. Add garlic and cook until lightly browned. Add broth and venison, then add carrots, potatoes, celery, tomato sauce, tomatoes, onion, soy sauce, Worcestershire sauce, rosemary, thyme, sage and cayenne pepper. Stir to mix thoroughly. Cook on low for 2 hours or until vegetables are done.

John Saboski
Trenton, New York

Venison Steaks in Green Peppercorn & Madeira Wine

Venison steaks
Ground pepper
Butter and oil (preferably macadamia nut oil)

Sauce
1 medium carrot, finely minced
2 T. butter
Olive oil or macadamia nut oil
1 small onion, finely minced
4 cloves garlic, finely minced
5 T. dry white wine
5 T. Madeira wine
1-oz. pkg. brown gravy mix, prepared according to instructions
1 T. Worcestershire sauce
4 bay leaves
½ tsp. thyme
½ tsp. rosemary
25 green peppercorns, whole
10 juniper berries, crushed
Salt

Microwave carrot to soften quickly; sauté in butter and oil with onion and garlic until onions are clear. Add wines, gravy, Worcestershire sauce, bay leaves, thyme, rosemary, peppercorns, berries and salt. Panfry steaks in pepper, butter and oil. Pour some sauce over each steak.

Note: Macadamia nut oil has a higher burning temperature and imparts a nutty flavor to the meat.

Scott R. Sabey
Salt Lake City, Utah

Venison Barley Soup

1 lb. venison stew meat, cut into 1-inch cubes,
    patted dry with paper towels
2 T. canola or vegetable oil
5 cups water
1 large onion, peeled and coarsely chopped
2 cloves garlic, peeled and minced
½ cup barley, rinsed
1 T. fresh oregano, chopped
1 tsp. salt
¼ tsp. freshly ground black pepper
2 medium carrots, peeled and thinly sliced
1 celery rib, sliced
1 small turnip, peeled and sliced
1 cup fresh or frozen peas
Brown gravy sauce (optional)

Heat oil in large soup pot over medium heat. Add venison and cook until well browned. Add water, onions, garlic, barley, oregano, salt and pepper. Heat to boiling; reduce heat to low, cover and simmer for 1 hour, stirring occasionally.

Skim fat if necessary; add remaining ingredients except peas. Simmer for 40 minutes or until vegetables are tender. Add peas and heat through. Add brown gravy sauce, if desired. Makes 3 quarts.

Gary Shaw
Enumclaw, Washington

Vinha D'Alaos
(Portuguese Pickled Liver)

2 lbs. venison liver
3 cloves garlic, each sliced in half
¼ tsp. Hawaiian red peppers, crushed
¾ cup cider vinegar
¾ cup water
1 tsp. Hawaiian salt (rock salt)
Flour
Oil

Slice liver and place in bowl. Combine garlic, red peppers, vinegar, water and salt; pour over liver and mix. Refrigerate for 2 days or longer, turning occasionally. Remove liver from liquid and roll in flour. Fry in hot oil.

Harvey Feuella
Haliimaile, Maui, Hawaii

Venison Barley Soup

GRANDMA'S VENISON MINCEMEAT

3 cups cooked venison, finely chopped
1 cup beef suet, finely chopped
6 cups apples, peeled, cored and chopped
1 cup raisins
1 cup currants
½ cup citron
½ cup chopped candied orange peel
2 cups packed brown sugar
½ cup molasses
¼ cup lemon juice
¼ cup cider vinegar
1 tsp. salt
½ tsp. cinnamon
½ tsp. nutmeg
½ tsp. ginger
¼ tsp. cloves
½ to 1 cup brandy

Mix meat, suet, apples, raisins, currants, citron, orange peel, brown sugar, molasses, lemon juice, vinegar and salt in a pot. Simmer for 2 hours.

Remove from heat and stir in cinnamon, nutmeg, ginger, cloves and brandy. Spoon into hot, clean jars; seal and keep in cold room or refrigerator up to 2 weeks before using. Makes enough for 4 (8- to 9-inch) pies.

Harvey J. Shippey
Acosta, Pennsylvania

BROTHER JOHN'S WATER-SMOKED BASIL-GARLIC VENISON RIB ROAST

2½ to 3½ lbs. venison rib roast
Italian seasoning
Ground white pepper
Rubbed sage
Dry meat seasoning, butcher-shop-style
1 bunch fresh basil leaves
6 cloves garlic, thinly sliced
8 slices bacon

Make sure rib bones are cut almost all the way through. Lightly season with mixture of Italian seasoning, white pepper, sage and meat seasoning. Chop half the basil and place it and half the garlic on meat side of roast. Cover with bacon and secure with wooden toothpicks. Let stand in refrigerator for 4 hours.

Place in water smoker. Place remaining basil and garlic in water pan and cook for 2½ to 3 hours. Use mesquite briquettes for best flavor. Keep water pan filled and keep heat range in the upper end of ideal.

Rick Wentworth
Clearlake, California

Rev. Brendan McGuire's Venison Roast

6 to 7 lbs. venison roast
1 large onion, chopped
2 T. chopped green onions
2 large carrots, chopped
5 T. butter or margarine
2 whole cloves
½ tsp. thyme
½ tsp. marjoram
½ tsp. tarragon
½ tsp. basil
½ tsp. rosemary
2 cups dry red wine, divided
Olive oil
Salt
Freshly ground black pepper
½ lb. salt pork
2 cloves garlic, cut into slivers
1 cup red currant jelly
Pinch of ginger
Pinch of cloves
1 tsp. lemon juice
¼ cup sour cream
Flour (if necessary)
1 T. brandy

Sauté onions and carrots in butter or margarine. Add cloves, thyme, marjoram, tarragon, basil and rosemary. Add 1 cup wine; put mixture through coarse sieve. Brush venison with olive oil; dust with plenty of salt and pepper. Cover venison with marinade pulp and liquid and soak for 12 to 24 hours. Lard venison generously with salt pork; insert slivers of garlic into venison. Place roast in oven bag. Pour marinade over meat, putting onions and carrots on top. Bake for 20 to 30 minutes per pound at 400°F, following baking bag instructions.

To make gravy: In saucepan, slowly melt jelly in drippings from oven bag. Add remaining 1 cup wine and simmer, adding ginger and cloves. Let thicken and reduce in volume a bit. Slowly add lemon juice and sour cream; mix thoroughly. If desired, thicken with flour. Just before serving, add brandy. Serve over wild or brown rice.

William Wewers
Clarksville, Arizona

Teriyaki Venison Steak

1 to 5 lbs. venison steak
¾ cup vegetable oil
¼ cup soy sauce
¼ cup sugar
2 T. vinegar
2 T. onion salt
1 tsp. garlic salt
1½ tsp. ginger

Combine oil, soy sauce, sugar, vinegar, onion salt, garlic salt and ginger. Pour over steak in glass bowl. Marinate for 6 to 12 hours in refrigerator. (I use a large zip-top bag for all marinating because there is no cleanup.) Cook as desired.

Monte Knight
Huntington, Vermont

MICROWAVE VENISON STROGANOFF

2 lbs. venison, thinly sliced to ⅛ x
    2-inch strips
⅔ cup butter, divided
1 medium onion, chopped
½ lb. fresh mushrooms, sliced or 8-
    oz. can sliced mushrooms
2 (10¾-oz.) cans cream of mush-
    room soup
8 oz. sour cream

Melt ⅓ cup butter in microwave-safe bowl. Add onions and mushrooms; microwave on high for 3 minutes; set aside. In 2-quart casserole, melt remaining ⅓ cup butter. Add venison and stir. Cover and microwave on high for 9 minutes, stirring every 3 minutes. Stir in onions, mushrooms and soup. Microwave on medium (50 percent power) for 12 to 15 minutes, stirring every 3 to 4 minutes. Stir in sour cream and microwave on high for 3 to 4 minutes. Serve over cooked noodles, rice or baked potatoes.

Tom Ostby
Rochester, Minnesota

VENISON STEAKS WITH FIRE WATER

2 to 3 lbs. venison steaks
¼ tsp. salt
½ tsp. garlic salt
1 tsp. dried minced onion
⅛ tsp. pepper
1 T. lemon juice
¼ cup Fire Water (recipe below)
½ cup dry red wine
10¾-oz. can cream of mushroom soup

FIRE WATER
(CAN SUBSTITUTE IN RECIPES CALLING FOR "WATER")
4 or 5 jalapeño peppers
2 large cloves garlic
1 sprig fresh oregano
1 bay leaf
½ tsp. cumin seed
1 tsp. salt
2 cups boiling water
Dried red pepper flakes (optional)

Brown steaks on both sides; place in casserole. In mixing bowl, combine salt, garlic salt, onion, pepper, lemon juice, Fire Water, wine and soup; pour over steaks. Bake, uncovered, for 30 to 45 minutes at 350°F or until done.

Wash and slice peppers; no need to remove seeds. Peel and slice garlic. Put oregano, bay leaf and cumin seed into clean jar. Add peppers, garlic and salt. Pour boiling water into jar. Cover and let stand for 24 hours. Strain out solids. Pour Fire Water into glass bottle, adding a few dried pepper flakes. Refrigerate between uses. Drizzle Fire Water over cooked chicken or meat. Sprinkle over cooked vegetables. Dip crusty bread into it. Add to soups or stews.

Mickey Kraft
May City, Iowa

HONEY ROAST VENISON

4-lb. venison roast
4 T. butter
½ cup honey, divided
6 to 8 slices bacon
1 onion, diced
1 tsp. soy sauce
1 clove garlic or ¼ tsp. garlic powder
Salt
Pepper
Small potatoes
Vegetables of choice

Melt butter in deep cast-iron kettle or Dutch oven. Sear roast. Add ¼ cup honey and sear roast again. Place bacon slices over roast; add onions and soy sauce. Add remaining ¼ cup of honey. Season with garlic, salt and pepper to taste. Add 1 cup water, cover and bake for 1½ hours at 225°F. Add potatoes and other vegetables, plus 1 cup water and return to oven, checking periodically, until potatoes are tender.

Howard Lofkvist
Cambridge, Minnesota

VENISON SAUERBRATEN

3½ to 4 lbs. deer, elk or moose shoulder roast, bottom round or rump roast
2 T. vegetable oil
3 medium red or green cabbages, cut into 8 wedges
15 gingersnap cookies, finely crushed
2 tsp. sugar

MARINADE
6 cups water
1 large onion, sliced
2 tsp. salt
10 whole black peppercorns
10 whole juniper berries (optional)
6 whole cloves
1 bay leaf
½ cup vinegar

To make marinade: In large saucepan, combine water, onion, salt, peppercorns, juniper berries, cloves, and bay leaf. Heat to boiling. Add vinegar. Cool slightly (about 10 minutes). Place meat in large glass or ceramic mixing bowl and cover with mixture. Cover tightly with plastic wrap and refrigerate for 2 to 3 days, turning meat once a day.

Remove meat from marinade, reserving liquid. In Dutch oven, brown roast on all sides in oil over medium heat. Add reserved liquid, reduce heat, cover and cook over low heat for 2 to 3 hours or until tender. Heat oven to 175°F just before meat is tender. With slotted spoon, transfer roast to oven-proof serving platter. Keep warm in oven.

Strain cooking liquid into 2-quart measuring cup. Add water if necessary to equal 5 cups. Return liquid to Dutch oven. Heat to boiling. Add cabbage wedges. Return to boil, reduce heat and cover. Simmer for 15 to 20 minutes or until cabbage is tender. With slotted spoon, transfer cabbage to platter with meat. In small bowl, combine crushed gingersnaps and sugar. Stir into liquid in Dutch oven. Cook over low heat, stirring occasionally, until bubbly and slightly thickened. Serve gingersnap sauce with roast and cabbage wedges. Makes 6 to 8 servings.

Vince Stracke
TyTy, Georgia

MEDALLIONS OF VENISON MARSALA

1 lb. venison loin, sliced into thin medallions
5 T. butter or margarine, divided
2 T. olive oil
¼ cup green onion tops, chopped fine
¼ cup Marsala wine
¼ cup beef stock
6 oz. morel mushrooms (fresh or dried)
Salt
Freshly ground pepper
Cornstarch
Water

In heavy skillet, heat 2 tablespoons butter with olive oil until it foams. Add medallions and fry for 3 to 4 minutes on each side. Remove meat from skillet to warm platter. Add remaining 3 tablespoons butter and toss in onion tops; sauté for 1 minute. Add wine and boil while scraping skillet to deglaze meat juices. Add beef stock and mushrooms. Simmer until mushrooms are tender; season with salt and pepper. Return steaks to skillet; heat through. Add cornstarch mixed with water to thicken slightly. Serve over noodles or with baked sweet potatoes.

Marlin E. Hartman
Indiana, Pennsylvania

Medallions of Venison Marsala

Venison Candy Appetizer

3 lbs. venison cuttings, tough steak or
    freezer surprise
1 cup soy sauce
1 cup good red wine
½ cup packed brown sugar
4 cloves garlic, chopped
Ground black pepper
Sage

Trim all fat and silver skin from meat. Cut meat into long, thin finger strips. Mix soy sauce, wine, brown sugar, garlic, pepper and sage; add meat. Cover and refrigerate for 48 hours, turning occasionally. Set grill on high and cook lightly on each side; do not overcook. Serve immediately as an appetizer. Meat will be tender, sweet and flavorful.

Clayton Moore
Langley, British Columbia, Canada

Venison Swiss Steak

1½ to 2 lbs. venison steak, cut
    1 inch thick
Flour
Salt
Pepper
2 T. cooking oil
1 medium onion, chopped fine
1 cup burgundy wine
10¾-oz. can cream of mushroom soup
½ soup can water
4-oz. can mushroom pieces, drained

Cut steak into serving-size pieces. Season flour with salt and pepper; sprinkle onto steak and pound in with meat mallet to ½ inch thick. Brown steak slowly in hot oil. Add onions and cook until onions are transparent. Place steak and onions in shallow 2½-quart baking dish. Add wine; cover and bake for 1 hour at 350°F. Add soup mixed with water and mushroom pieces. Return to oven and bake for 45 to 60 minutes or until steak is fork tender. Thicken juices for gravy, if desired.

Laura Point
Submitted by grandson Jon Point
Deer River, Minnesota

Grape Herb Sauce for Venison

4 T. butter
½ cup grape jelly
½ tsp. dried herbs (your choice)

Melt butter and jelly; blend in herbs. Serve in small pitcher to pour over venison roast.

William Ostermeyer
Kilbourne, Illinois

Italian Venison Stew

2 lbs. venison, cubed and browned in oil
2 small zucchini, peeled and cubed
2 carrots, sliced ⅛ inch thick
8 plum tomatoes, peeled and cubed
6 celery ribs, sliced
1 large onion, coarsely chopped
½ lb. mushrooms, coarsely chopped
8 cups beef bouillon
2 T. parsley flakes
¼ tsp. savory
¼ tsp. thyme
½ tsp. salt
¼ tsp. black pepper
Worcestershire sauce
Tabasco sauce
Parmesan cheese

In Crock-Pot set on high, combine venison, zucchini, carrots, tomatoes, celery, onion, mushrooms, bouillon, parsley flakes, savory, thyme, salt and pepper; mix well. Stir in Worcestershire sauce and Tabasco sauce to taste. Cook for 4 to 5 hours or until carrots are tender. Serve with grated Parmesan cheese sprinkled on top. This is especially great for those on low-carbohydrate diets.

Randal Exley
Wexford, Pennsylvania

Venison Schnitzels (Cutlets)
with Portobello Mushroom Sauce

8 cutlets from leg, about 3 oz. each
½ cup flour
2 eggs
1 cup bread crumbs
½ cup grated Parmesan cheese
3 T. butter
3 T. olive oil

Sauce
2 shallots, finely chopped
Garlic, finely chopped
4 cups sliced portobello mushrooms
1 cup red wine (Madeira or Port)
1 cup game or beef broth
½ cup whipping cream
Salt
Pepper
Fresh parsley

Pound meat with mallet between 2 sheets of plastic wrap (prevents meat from sticking to mallet) into ¼-inch-thick schnitzels, allowing 2 per person. Put flour in one bowl, beat eggs in another bowl and mix bread crumbs and Parmesan cheese in third bowl. Dredge each schnitzel in flour, shaking off excess, then in egg and finally in bread crumb mixture, pressing mixture into meat with hands. Heat butter and oil in skillet over medium heat. Fry schnitzels for 2 minutes on each side or until golden brown. Set aside in warm oven. Add butter and oil as needed to fry remaining schnitzels.

Scrape any breading from frying pan. Add shallots and garlic. Sauté for 1 minute. Add mushrooms and more butter, if needed. Sauté for a few minutes or until mushrooms soften. Deglaze pan with wine and boil down to half the volume. Add broth and heat to boiling. Reduce heat, add cream and simmer to creamy consistency, stirring frequently. Adjust seasoning with salt and pepper to taste. Place 2 schnitzels on each warmed plate, cover with sauce and garnish with fresh parsley. Complement with glazed baby carrots and perogies, pasta or rice.

Dave Jack
London, Ontario, Canada

Venison Liver Pâté

VENISON LIVER PÂTÉ

½ of a deer liver (about 1½ lbs.)
Milk
1 cup finely chopped onion
10 T. butter or margarine, divided
½ lb. fresh mushrooms or 2 (4-oz.) cans
2 tsp. seasoned salt
2 tsp. lemon juice
½ tsp. pepper
½ tsp. cayenne pepper
5 large hard-cooked eggs, peeled and quartered

Trim all fat and connecting tissue from liver. Slice to ⅓ inch thick. Soak in bowl of milk in refrigerator for about an hour. Rinse and pat dry; set aside.

Sauté onions in 5 tablespoons butter or margarine in large skillet until tender. Add mushrooms and liver; simmer until liver is done or just until "red" is out; do not overcook. Remove from heat and add remaining 5 tablespoons butter or margarine, seasoned salt, lemon juice, pepper and cayenne pepper. Let butter melt and stir mixture. Put about ⅕ of mixture and 1 quartered hard-boiled egg into blender and purée at high speed for about 30 seconds. Mixture should be as smooth as possible. Scoop into large bowl and continue process until all of mixture and eggs have been puréed. Stir entire batch together to get a consistent mix and scoop into 8-ounce plastic containers. Refrigerate for about 8 hours to allow mixture to firm up. (You'll probably be sampling out of the blender, so let your sense of taste tell you if the seasonings are balanced for you.) Mixture keeps for 8 to 10 days in refrigerator or in freezer for about a month. If using out of freezer, add 1 tablespoon of mayonnaise to smooth out consistency. Serve with your favorite crackers.

Edwin Willie
Mattawan, Michigan

VENISON LIVER À LA SCOTT

2 lbs. venison liver, cut into ½-inch-thick slices
8 oz. bacon, cut into 1-inch pieces
2 large onions, thinly sliced
Salt
Black pepper
3 to 5 T. balsamic vinegar
3 T. chicken stock

Fry bacon in large skillet until crisp. Remove with slotted spoon and set aside. Add onions to skillet and cook over medium heat for 20 to 25 minutes or until golden. Remove with slotted spoon and set aside.

Increase heat to medium-high. When bacon fat is hot, sauté liver, a few slices at a time. Do not overcook. Season with salt and pepper while cooking. Remove liver and keep warm. Add vinegar and stock to skillet and heat to boiling, scraping up any brown bits. Add onions and toss over medium heat for 30 seconds. Arrange liver on platter or individual plates; top with onions and reserved bacon. Pour remaining liquid over liver to serve.

Scott Westall
Roswell, Georgia

VENISON PICATTA

1¼ lbs. deer, antelope, elk or
    moose loin
2 cups milk, divided
½ cup flour
½ tsp. salt
½ tsp. pepper
¼ cup butter or margarine
¾ cup dry white wine
2 to 3 T. fresh lemon juice
¼ cup snipped fresh
    parsley
1 to 2 T. capers, drained

Slice loin across grain into thin slices ¼ inch thick or less. (Venison is easier to slice if partially frozen.) In shallow dish, combine meat and 1 cup milk. Cover dish with plastic wrap and place in refrigerator for 1 to 3 hours. Drain and discard milk. Add remaining 1 cup milk. Let stand at room temperature for 1 hour. Drain and discard milk. Pat venison slices dry with paper towel.

On sheet of waxed paper, mix flour, salt and pepper. Dip venison slices into flour mixture, turning to coat. In large skillet, melt butter over medium-high heat. Add venison slices; brown on both sides. Add wine; cook for about 2 minutes. Transfer venison to heated platter with slotted spoon. Add lemon juice, parsley and capers to skillet. Reduce heat to medium. Cook for about 2 minutes, stirring constantly and scraping bottom and sides of skillet. Serve sauce over venison slices.

Vince Stracke
TyTy, Georgia

SAVORY VENISON POT PIE

1½ lbs. venison, cut into chunks
4 T. flour, divided
¾ tsp. salt
½ tsp. pepper
2 T. cooking oil
2 medium onions, chopped
2 medium potatoes, cubed
1 medium carrot, diced
1¼ cups beer, divided
½ cup beef broth
2 T. tomato paste
1 bay leaf
½ tsp. dried, crushed thyme
1 double pie crust
Milk

Mix 3 tablespoons flour, salt and pepper; coat venison. Brown in hot oil; remove from pan. Sauté onions. Return meat to pan. Add potatoes, carrot, 1 cup beer, broth, tomato paste, bay leaf and thyme; mix well. Bring to a boil; reduce heat. Simmer for approximately 1 hour. Discard bay leaf. Prepare pastry crust. Mix remaining ¼ cup beer and remaining 1 tablespoon flour; add to meat mixture. Cook and stir until thickened and bubbly. Turn mix into pie shell. Cover with top pastry, slitting for steam to escape. Brush with milk. Place on baking sheet. Bake at 450°F for 20 to 30 minutes or until brown.

Edward Sibole
Gerrardstown, West Virginia

VENISON BACKSTRAPS

1 to 2 whole boneless backstraps
2 to 4 oz. Worcestershire sauce
2 oz. red wine vinegar
2 to 4 oz. soy sauce
4 oz. olive oil
2 T. hot sauce
2 T. minced garlic
1 onion, diced
1 T. oregano
1 T. onion powder
1 T. garlic powder
1 T. dried basil
1 T. parsley
1 tsp. black pepper or cayenne pepper
1 bay leaf

In large zip-top bag, mix Worcestershire sauce, vinegar, soy sauce, olive oil, hot sauce, garlic, onion, oregano, onion powder, garlic powder, basil, parsley, black pepper and bay leaf. Add meat and mix thoroughly. Refrigerate for 3 days. Shake each morning and night. Remove from marinade and grill over medium heat, turning every 5 minutes. Spoon marinade over meat after each turn. Do not use any marinade on the last turn. Grill for approximately 20 minutes or until meat is only slightly pink in center. Do not overcook. Remove meat and slice across grain in ¼-inch slices.

Mike Gaydas
South Plainfield, New Jersey

TERIYAKI VENISON STIR-FRY
WITH WILD RICE

1 to 1½ lbs. venison steak
3 T. olive oil or other cooking oil
1 large green bell pepper, sliced
1 small jalapeño pepper, sliced (optional)
2 cloves garlic, minced
1 small onion, chopped
8-oz. can mushrooms, drained
2 tsp. seasoned salt
1½ tsp. chili powder
¼ tsp. black pepper
¼ tsp. red pepper
1 cup thick teriyaki stir-fry and marinade sauce
1 T. soy sauce
1 T. Worcestershire sauce
1 T. packed brown sugar

Cut steak into bite-sized pieces. Heat oil in skillet on medium-high heat. Brown meat on all sides. Add green bell pepper, jalapeño pepper, garlic, onion, mushrooms, seasoned salt, chili powder, black pepper, red pepper, marinade sauce, soy sauce, Worcestershire sauce and brown sugar. Cook on medium-high heat to boil off all moisture, stirring frequently. It is done when sauce is sticky and very dark in color. Serve over wild rice.

Mike & Haley Hallstrom
Pender, Nebraska

Roadkill Chili

ROADKILL CHILI

9 lbs. wild game meat (venison, elk, Nilgai or a combination), cut into ¼- to ½-inch cubes
½ cup cooking oil
3 green peppers, chopped medium
3 yellow onions, chopped medium or 10 green onions
2 fresh jalapeño peppers, seeded and finely chopped
4 cloves garlic, chopped fine
3 oz. chili powder or cayenne pepper
1½ tsp. cumin seeds
1 oz. Tabasco sauce
7-oz. can diced green chiles
14-oz. can stewed tomatoes
3 (15-oz.) cans tomato sauce
6-oz. can tomato paste
12-oz. can beer
Water
Salt or seasoned salt
Pepper

Heat oil in large pot. Sauté peppers, onions, jalapeño peppers and garlic, stirring constantly. Add meat and brown lightly. Stir in chili powder or cayenne pepper, cumin, Tabasco sauce, green chiles, tomatoes, tomato sauce, tomato paste and beer. Cover with about an inch of water. Season to taste and let bubble slowly for 3 to 5 hours or until meat is tender and sauce is thick. After 2 hours, skim off fat, taste and season more, if necessary.

Note: *This chili's odd name reflects the power of its spices, not the quality of meat you should use.*

Clair A. Glantz
Pueblo, Colorado

Oriental-Style Grilled Venison Ribs

2 to 3 lbs. deer, antelope, elk or moose ribs
¼ cup peanut oil or vegetable oil
¼ cup rice wine vinegar
⅓ cup plus 1 scant T. soy sauce
1½ cups dry sherry
6 T. plum sauce or 3 T. plum jelly
2 T. hoisin sauce
3 T. minced fresh gingerroot
4 cloves garlic, minced

In medium saucepan, combine oil, vinegar, soy sauce, sherry, plum sauce, hoisin sauce, gingerroot and garlic. Cook over medium heat, stirring constantly, until hot. Cool to room temperature. Place ribs in 13 x 9-inch glass baking pan or oven cooking bag. Pour cooled marinade over ribs. Cover pan with plastic wrap or seal bag. Marinate ribs for 1 to 2 hours, turning several times. Preheat grill. Cook ribs for 10 to 15 minutes, turning once. Serve with remaining sauce.

Vince Stracke
TyTy, Georgia

Venison Parmigiana

1 lb. venison round
   steak or loin
½ cup Italian bread
   crumbs
¼ cup finely grated
   Parmesan cheese
1¼ tsp. salt or garlic salt
⅛ tsp. pepper
1 egg, slightly beaten
⅓ cup olive oil
28-oz. jar meatless
   spaghetti sauce
½ lb. coarsely grated
   mozzarella cheese

Remove all fat and membrane from meat; cut ½ inch thick and into serving-size pieces (about 3 pieces per steak). Pound thin. Mix bread crumbs, Parmesan cheese, salt and pepper. Dip venison in egg, then crumbs to coat, patting crumbs on venison so they stick firmly. Arrange venison on wire rack and let dry for 10 to 12 minutes so coating will adhere during cooking. Heat oil in heavy skillet over moderately high heat for about 1 minute. Add half of venison and brown for 1 to 1½ minutes per side. Brown remaining venison. Arrange venison in single layer on slightly greased pizza pan. Bake, uncovered, for 20 to 25 minutes.

In saucepan, heat spaghetti sauce. Spoon heated sauce on top of each piece and sprinkle mozzarella cheese on top of sauce. Return to oven for 5 to 10 minutes or until mozzarella cheese is melted. Serve with spaghetti or mostaccioli topped with remaining spaghetti sauce, garlic bread and tossed salad.

Note: Place frozen meat on wire rack in pan and cover. Thaw for 3 to 4 days in refrigerator. This will remove excess blood and keep breading crisp when frying.

Richard Miller
Westfield, Wisconsin

Oriental-Style Grilled Venison Ribs

Hot Pepper Venison Stir-Fry

1 to 1½ lbs. venison loin or other steak
4 T. (½ stick) butter (more if needed)
½ large green or red pepper
1 yellow hot wax pepper or other hot pepper (the hotter the better)
½ medium onion, chopped
½ to 1 cup chopped mushrooms
2 T. garlic powder
1 tsp. cayenne pepper
2 T. seasoned salt
2 T. Worcestershire sauce
1 T. Texas Pete hot sauce
10½-oz. can beef gravy

Combine butter, peppers, onion and mushrooms in large skillet; sauté. Add garlic powder and cayenne pepper. Add venison and cook over medium heat. Mix in seasoned salt, Worcestershire sauce and hot sauce. While meat is simmering, heat gravy. When meat is thoroughly cooked, pour over plate of hot rice and top with gravy. If desired, top with more hot sauce.

Marc Lauber
Hollidaysburg, Pennsylvania

Braised Venison in Sour Cream

2 lbs. venison
¼ cup bacon fat
1 clove garlic, chopped
1 cup diced celery
1 cup diced carrots
½ cup minced onion
2 cups water
1 bay leaf
1 cup tart fruit juice (apple or grapefruit)
8 peppercorns
1 tsp. salt
4 T. butter
4 T. flour
1 cup sour cream

Wipe meat with clean damp cloth, then cut into 2-inch pieces. Melt bacon fat in heavy frying pan. Add meat and garlic; sauté until brown on all sides. Arrange meat in 2-quart casserole. Put celery, carrots and onions in frying pan and cook for 2 minutes in remaining bacon grease. Add water, bay leaf, juice, peppercorns and salt. Pour mixture over meat and bake at 325°F for 30 to 60 minutes or until meat is tender. Drain liquid from casserole and set aside. Melt butter in frying pan. Stir in flour; blend. Add liquid from casserole, stirring constantly until mixture thickens and boils. Add sour cream and more salt, if necessary; mix well. Heat to boiling. Pour over meat and vegetables in casserole. Remove bay leaf before serving. Serve immediately with buttered noodles and peach, plum or currant jelly.

Ray Murley
Oshawa, Ontario, Canada

Franconian Summer Game
(German-Style)

3 lbs. venison roast
4 T. butter
2 medium red onions, diced
3 medium carrots, diced
½ bunch celery, diced
Salt
Pepper
Marjoram
Thyme
1 cup broth (venison, beef, etc.)
3 T. red wine

Marinade
Raspberry vinegar
Water
Salt
Sugar

Garnish
Romaine lettuce
Sliced hard-cooked egg
Sliced sweet green pepper
Diced onions
Chopped fresh chives
Pink peppercorns
Pumpkin seed oil, sunflower oil or light olive oil
Fresh parsley

Melt butter in skillet. Add red onions, carrots and celery; brown lightly. Place vegetables on bottom of lightly oiled roasting pan or Dutch oven. Place venison on top of vegetables; season liberally with salt, pepper, marjoram and thyme. Pour broth then wine over meat. Cover and bake at 350°F for 3 to 4 hours or until thoroughly cooked.

Remove meat from oven and allow to cool completely. When room temperature, slice thinly across grain. Make a bed of romaine leaves on platter and arrange venison slices neatly on top. Arrange slices of hard-cooked egg, green pepper, diced onion, chives and pink peppercorns on platter with meat to add color and extra flavor.

Blend a few tablespoons of raspberry vinegar and a little water with a pinch or two of salt and sugar. Drizzle over meat. Just before serving sprinkle pumpkin seed oil over whole platter. Garnish with fresh parsley. Guten Appetit und Weidmannsheil!

G. F. Hohenberger Jr.
New York, New York

Laurie's Venison Surprise

3 lbs. venison steaks or chops, cubed
1 cup flour
1 T. salt
1 tsp. pepper
1 tsp. Italian seasoning
Olive oil
2 (4-oz.) cans mushrooms, sliced
14-oz. can artichoke hearts in oil
½ medium onion, diced

Mix flour, salt, pepper and Italian seasoning. Coat venison with flour mixture. Heat olive oil and brown meat for 4 to 5 minutes on each side. Add mushrooms, artichoke hearts and onion; fry until vegetables begin to brown, stirring so meat does not overcook. Add more olive oil if mixture begins to dry out. Serve over cooked spaghetti; garnish with Parmesan cheese.

Norm & Laurie Maxwell
Manchester, Michigan

Chapter 2
BIG GAME

Elk, boar, bear, pronghorn, moose, caribou and more ... these great recipes honor the variety of big game beyond venison that we bring home. Keep in mind that many of the culinary ideas here are interchangeable with other big game meat; it's the ideas that count the most, and that you need the most.

Hawaiian Wild Boar (Adobo)

4 lbs. wild boar, cut into 1 to 2-inch pieces
Olive oil
5 potatoes, cut into 1 to 2-inch pieces
4 cloves garlic, mashed
1 tsp. peppercorns
5 bay leaves
1½ cups vinegar or enough to cover meat
4 T. soy sauce (optional)
1 T. Hawaiian sea salt
1 T. Hawaiian cane sugar
½ cup hot water (optional)

Brown meat with a little olive oil in large pot. Combine potatoes, garlic, peppercorns, bay leaves, vinegar, soy sauce, sea salt and cane sugar; add mixture to browned meat. Bring to a boil, then reduce heat and simmer with cover slightly ajar until meat is tender and ¾ of liquid evaporates.

If meat is still tough and there is no more stock, add hot water and continue simmering. Serve with steamed rice.

Note: Pheasant may be substituted for boar meat.

Pat Rapozo
Lihue, Hawaii

Baked Elk Steak

1 or 2 elk steaks, ¾ inch thick
1 medium onion, chopped
10¾-oz. can golden mushroom soup

Remove any bone, fat and muscle covering from meat. Place steaks in 9 x 12-inch baking pan. Spread onion on top. Pour soup over top. Cover pan and bake for 1 1/2 hours at 350°F.

John Klingenberg
Zeeland, Michigan

Barbecued Elk, Moose, Wild Boar or Venison Ribs

Rack of ribs
2 T. dry mustard
⅓ cup chili sauce
1 cup packed brown sugar
¾ cup pineapple juice
1 tsp. lemon juice

Mix dry mustard, chili sauce, brown sugar, pineapple juice and lemon juice. Allow to simmer, covered, for a few minutes. Brush over ribs and grill until done. Also good on game birds.

William Ostermeyer
Kilbourne, Illinois

ELK STEAK SICILIANO

Elk steaks (backstraps, tenderloins, sirloin, top or
    bottom round) or substitute your favorite venison,
    boar, chicken, quail, pheasant, beef, pig or fish
Extra virgin olive oil
Coarsely ground pepper
Garlic powder
Salt
8- to 15-oz. pkg. Progresso Italian Bread Crumbs

Trim meat of all fat and sinew, then slice into steaks about $1\frac{1}{2}$ to $2\frac{1}{2}$ inches thick (appropriate thickness is important).

Put 1 cup olive oil into large mixing bowl. Place meat in oil, one piece at a time, coating completely. Set meat on waxed paper. Repeat for all steaks, using more oil as necessary. Sprinkle all steaks lightly with coarsely ground pepper, garlic powder and salt; turn steaks and repeat.

Place bread crumbs in separate large mixing bowl. Roll steaks into bread crumbs, coating completely, and place flat onto foil-covered baking sheet. Use more bread crumbs if necessary. When all steaks are on sheet, drizzle a small amount of extra oil on top of breaded steaks, if desired (be careful not to use too much).

Preheat oven to broil. When ready, place baking sheet on bottom shelf of oven and cook steaks for 7 minutes. Flip steaks over. Cook for an additional 7 minutes. (To avoid tough meat, do not overcook.) Lightly salt top; serve immediately.

Guide: A $1\frac{1}{2}$-inch steak will be medium rare, a $2\frac{1}{2}$-inch elk/venison steak medium rare with rare in the center. This meat will continue to cook by itself as it sits, and after about 3 minutes the $1\frac{1}{2}$-inch steak will be nicely medium rare (light pink inside) to medium (faintest pink inside); the $2\frac{1}{2}$-inch steak will be medium rare in the center to medium on the edges.

Gary Johnson
Shelby Township, MI

IDIOT-PROOF CROCK-POT STEW

1 to 2 lbs. elk or venison, cut into bite-size pieces
1 cup sliced carrots
2 cups cubed potatoes
1 cup green peas
1 cup snapped green beans
2 cups water
2 (1-oz.) pkgs. brown gravy mix
1 T. pressed garlic
Salt
Pepper

Mix elk or venison in large Crock-Pot with carrots, potatoes, peas, beans, water, gravy mix, garlic, salt and pepper. Cook on high for approximately 8 hours. If you anticipate cooking longer than 8 hours, use the low setting.

Daniel W. Poole
Chester, Virginia

CARIBOU HEART STROGANOFF

1 caribou heart, ¼-inch slices
Olive oil or bacon drippings
12-oz. pkg. noodles
½ cup minced onion
½ cup milk (or equivalent made from powder)
1 tsp. black pepper
2 pkgs. stroganoff mix
½ cup dried mushrooms
½ cup dried peas or corn
1 tsp. salt
1 tsp. Italian seasoning
½ tsp. garlic powder
4 slices cheese or equivalent

Stir-fry sliced heart in olive oil until red meat turns slightly brown. Add 7 cups water, noodles, onion, milk, pepper, stroganoff mix, mushrooms, peas or corn, salt, Italian seasoning and garlic powder. Heat to boiling and simmer for 8 minutes, stirring occasionally. Add cheese, stir and let stand for 5 minutes. Thin with water, if desired.

Note: This is a great recipe for fly-in drop camp hunting. Caribou heart is very tender compared to regular meat cuts and is tasty as well. It will cook much faster than steak cuts and won't be tough.

Frank Scholtz
Rancho Palos Verdes, California

MOUNTAIN LION CASSEROLE

1 lion loin, boned and browned
1.4-oz. pkg. onion soup mix
10¾-oz. can cream of mushroom soup
Wine

Place loin in covered casserole. Add onion soup mix, mushroom soup and enough wine to cover. Bake at 350ºF for 45 to 60 minutes or until done.

Note: Mountain lion meat is white and quite similar to pork, but very dry. Be sure to keep dish at least half full of liquids.

O. J. Utton
Chama, New Mexico

Bear Roast

5- to 6-lb. bear roast
4 cups water
1 T. salt
½ cup vinegar
3 strips thick sliced bacon or salt pork
1 large onion, quartered
¼ cup butter, melted
1 tsp. salt
¼ tsp. pepper

Trim all fat from roast; wash well. Soak meat for at least 2 hours in water, salt and vinegar. Remove and pat dry. Place meat in roaster, lay strips of bacon on top, and place onion beside it. Roast in oven for 3 hours at 350°F. About 15 minutes before serving, remove bacon strips. Coat top of roast with butter. Sprinkle with salt and pepper. Roast for another 15 minutes and baste with butter during this time. Serve hot.

Note: Bear meat is usually rich, tender and delicious, especially if the animal is under 3 years old. Meat from older animals may need to be tenderized by marinating for 24 hours. The gamey flavor that some people find objectionable is concentrated in the fat, so trim the fat from the meat before cooking. Bear meat is not marbled with fat like top-grade beef, so roasts and larger cuts should be larded. This is done by piercing meat several times and inserting thin strips of chilled salt pork into the slits, or fastening strips of fat around the meat with a string.

Wayne Wright
Surrey, British Columbia, Canada

Barbecued Bear

3 lbs. bear steak, trimmed and cut into 2-inch cubes
1 slice salt pork, cut up
1 cup ketchup
⅓ cup steak sauce
2 T. tarragon vinegar
1 onion, diced
1 T. lemon juice
1 tsp. salt
1 T. chili powder

Sear meat on all sides with salt pork in heavy frying pan. Place meat in casserole. Mix ketchup, steak sauce, vinegar, onion, lemon juice, salt and chili powder in frying pan and bring to a boil, stirring constantly. Pour sauce over meat. Cover and bake for 2 hours at 325°F or until meat is tender. Stir occasionally.

Harvey Shippey
Acosta, Pennsylvania

SAUTÉED ELK STEAKS
WITH FRESH MUSHROOMS & SHERRY-CREAM SAUCE

2 lbs. elk or other venison steaks
2 T. butter
½ lb. fresh chanterelle or morel mushrooms, brushed clean and sliced
½ lb. button or cremini mushrooms, brushed clean and sliced
¼ cup dry sherry
¾ cup heavy cream
1 cup flour
1¼ tsp. salt, divided
½ tsp. freshly ground black pepper
2 T. vegetable oil or mild olive oil

Heat butter in large, heavy skillet and sauté mushrooms for several minutes over medium heat until soft and browned. Pour in sherry and cream and cook for about 10 minutes or until cream starts to thicken and turns a light brown. Meanwhile, blend flour, 1 teaspoon salt and pepper. Dredge steaks in flour mixture and set aside. In another skillet large enough to hold steaks comfortably, heat oil to medium-hot and cook steaks for 3 to 4 minutes on each side. Season mushrooms and sauce with remaining ¼ teaspoon salt and serve over cooked steaks.

Gary Shaw
Enumclaw, Washington

CREAMY WILD HOG DIP

1 lb. wild boar sausage
4 fresh jalapeño peppers
10-oz. can tomatoes with green chiles
1 lb. cream cheese

Dice jalapeño peppers and brown with sausage. Add tomatoes and simmer for 2 to 3 minutes. Add cream cheese and heat until fully melted; stirring to mix. Serve hot with tortilla chips.

Jeremy Gregory
Russellville, Arkansas

WILD BOAR STEW

1 lb. boar meat, boned and cubed
½ lb. bacon
1 onion, chopped
1 tsp. crushed garlic
2 tsp. curry powder
½ cup water, divided
2 T. parsley flakes
16-oz. can stewed tomatoes
¼ cup sliced carrots
2 medium potatoes, cubed
2 T. cornstarch

Fry bacon in skillet until crisp. Remove bacon; cool, crumble and set aside. Pour off all but 3 tablespoons bacon grease. Cook boar meat with onion, garlic and curry powder in remaining grease until meat is browned, stirring frequently. Stir in ¼ cup water. Remove from heat and set aside. In 2-quart casserole, combine parsley, stewed tomatoes, carrots and potatoes. Add meat mixture and mix well. Bake for 30 minutes at 350°F. Mix cornstarch with remaining ¼ cup water and stir into casserole. Bake for another 30 minutes or until meat and vegetables are tender.

Brandon McKinniss
Harker Heights, Texas

Sautéed Elk Steaks with Fresh Mushrooms & Sherry-Cream Sauce

Ragout of Moose (or Deer)

3 lbs. shoulder or any other cut
2 cups red wine
¼ cup cider
2 large onions, thinly sliced
2 carrots, sliced
6 peppercorns, ground
2 bay leaves
2 cloves
1 clove garlic
½ tsp. thyme
1 T. salt
3 T. bacon fat
2 T. flour
2 celery ribs and leaves, chopped
4 carrots, sliced
12 to 15 chestnuts, brown peeling removed (optional)
Salt
Pepper

Remove excess fat from meat and cut into 2-inch lengths. Mix wine, cider, onions, carrots, ground peppercorns, bay leaves, cloves, garlic, thyme and salt in non-aluminum bowl. Add meat and stir. Cover and refrigerate for 2 days.

Remove meat from marinade, reserving marinade. Strain marinade and set aside. Pat meat dry, then brown in bacon fat. Dredge meat with flour and place in Dutch oven or stockpot. Cover with reserved marinade; add celery, carrots and chestnuts. Season with salt and pepper. Cover and simmer for 2 hours. Serve with mashed potatoes.

Wayne Wright
Surrey, British Columbia, Canada

Moose Liver in White Wine

1 lb. moose liver, sliced
1 cup flour
4 T. olive oil
1 small red onion, minced
2 cloves garlic, crushed
Salt
Pepper
½ cup white wine

Dredge liver in flour and brown slowly in olive oil in cast-iron frying pan. Set aside in warm pan. Sauté onion and garlic in same cast-iron frying pan for approximately 5 minutes; return liver to pan and spoon onion and garlic over top of liver. Season with salt and pepper; pour wine over top. Cover with foil and cook slowly for 30 minutes, basting occasionally.

Roger Laye
Prince George, British Columbia, Canada

Saucy Elk Steak Skillet

1 lb. elk or venison steak, cut into serving pieces
¼ cup flour
1 T. olive oil
1 cup chopped onion
1 cup water
¼ cup ketchup
1 T. Worcestershire sauce
¼ cup diced green bell pepper
1 tsp. beef bouillon granules
1 tsp. salt
¼ tsp. pepper
½ tsp. dried marjoram leaves
10-oz. pkg. frozen green beans
3 to 4 medium potatoes, boiled, peeled, cooled and
    sliced
1 cup canned tomatoes

Coat steak pieces with flour; pound into steak. Brown in hot oil in 10-inch skillet; push steak to side. Cook and stir onion in oil until tender; drain.

Mix water, ketchup, Worcestershire sauce, green bell pepper, bouillon, salt, pepper and marjoram; pour over steak and onion. Heat to boiling; reduce heat. Cover and simmer for 45 minutes to 1 hour or until steak is tender, stirring 2 or 3 times.

Rinse frozen beans to separate. Add beans, potatoes and tomatoes to skillet. Heat to boiling; reduce heat. Cover and simmer for 10 to 15 minutes or until beans are tender.

Marlin E. Hartman
Indiana, Pennsylvania

Elk Parmesan

1½ lbs. elk steak
Garlic salt
Pepper
1½ cups Italian bread crumbs
½ cups grated Parmesan cheese
2 eggs
¼ cup water
¼ cup olive oil
1½ cups spaghetti sauce, divided
6 slices mozzarella cheese

Cut meat into 6 pieces; pound with tenderizer. Sprinkle with garlic salt and pepper. In mixing bowl, combine bread crumbs and Parmesan cheese. In separate bowl, beat eggs with water. Dip both sides of meat in egg, then into bread crumb mixture. Refrigerate for 20 minutes.

Heat oil in large skillet. Brown meat on both sides. Place in greased 13 x 9 x 2-inch baking pan. Spoon 2 tablespoons spaghetti sauce over each piece. Cover with mozzarella cheese. Top with spaghetti sauce. Bake, uncovered, for 30 minutes at 350ºF or until tender. Serve over noodles with parsley garnish. Makes 6 servings.

Kimberly Kothman
Iraan, Texas

20-Below Moose Stew

20-Below Moose Stew

3 lbs. stew meat (moose or other big game)
Oil
1 cup water
2 T. packed brown sugar
¼ tsp. thyme
1 T. paprika
1 tsp. cinnamon
¼ tsp. sage
2 tsp. beef bouillon granules
3 to 4 onions
1 clove garlic
4 to 5 potatoes
6 to 8 carrots
2 to 3 turnips
1 bay leaf
3 cups barley
1 T. salt
1 tsp. pepper
2 cups peas
2 cups green beans
2 cups corn
2 cups mushrooms
¼ cup butter
¼ cup flour

Remove silver skin from meat and cut into ¾-inch cubes. Carefully brown meat in oil on medium high heat; remove from heat. Simmer 1 cup water, brown sugar, thyme, paprika, cinnamon, sage and bouillon. Microwave onions and garlic until tender; add to meat. Microwave potatoes, carrots and turnips in covered dish for 7 minutes on high; add to stew pot. Add meat, bay leaf, barley, salt, pepper and enough water to cover all. Add peas, beans, corn and mushrooms. Melt butter in saucepan and blend in flour; add to stew pot. Simmer for 2 to 3 hours, stirring occasionally.

Phillip Scheller
Del Rio, Texas

CORNED MOOSE ROAST

1 large moose roast
1 cup curing salt
1 T. black peppercorns
1 T. whole cloves or allspice
3 carrots, peeled and cut into large chunks
3 celery ribs with leaves, cut into large chunks
1 medium onion, cut into chunks
6 to 8 small to medium red potatoes
1 lb. baby carrots
1 medium head of cabbage, cut into large chunks

In large glass or stainless steel bowl, mix curing salt with enough water to cover roast; add roast. Cover with plastic wrap and refrigerate for 5 to 6 days, turning once a day. Discard marinade. Place roast in large kettle with peppercorns, cloves or allspice, carrots, celery and onion. Add enough water to cover all. Bring to a boil in covered kettle. Reduce heat and simmer for 3½ to 4 hours or until tender.

Strain and discard vegetables and seasonings; reserve broth. Add potatoes, baby carrots, cabbage and enough of the reserved broth to cover all. Cook for 30 minutes or until vegetables are tender. Serve hot for regular meal; also makes excellent cold meat sandwiches.

Kate Hoppe
Powell, Wyoming

BEAR ROAST WITH RHUBARB MEAT SAUCE

4- to 5-lb. bear roast
1 T. rosemary
1 T. minced garlic
1 T. sage
½ cup red wine
2 cups water

RHUBARB MEAT SAUCE
16-oz. pkg. rhubarb
½ cup chopped onion
1 cup raisins
2 cups packed brown sugar
¼ cup vinegar
1 tsp. salt
1 tsp. ginger
1 tsp. cinnamon
1 tsp. allspice

Place meat in roaster. Add rosemary, garlic, sage, wine and water. Cover tightly. Bake for 3 to 4 hours at 350°F, turning meat every hour. Serve with Rhubarb Meat Sauce (below).

In large pot, mix rhubarb, onion, raisins, brown sugar, vinegar and salt. Heat to boiling. Simmer for 25 minutes, stirring frequently. Add ginger, cinnamon and allspice; cook for 5 minutes.

Marge Woods
Submitted by William R. Lee
Stockbridge, Georgia

Will's Wild Liver Skillet

1 to 2 lbs. elk or venison liver, skinned and sliced
2 cups flour
½ tsp. salt
½ tsp. pepper
1 lb. bacon
1 to 2 large onions, sliced
10¾-oz. can cream of mushroom, celery or onion soup
8-oz. can sliced mushrooms or fresh mushrooms (optional)

In zip-top bag, mix flour, salt and pepper. Coat liver with flour mixture. Fry bacon in large skillet; set aside. Quickly brown liver in bacon grease. When all pieces are browned, drain off any remaining grease. In same skillet, layer liver, onion and bacon. Mix soup, mushrooms and enough water to cover. Cover skillet and simmer for 20 to 30 minutes.

William Miller
Fond du Lac, Wisconsin

Barbecued Elk, Moose or Venison

3 lbs. wild game meat
1.4-oz. pkg. dry onion soup mix
½ cup ketchup
½ (16-oz.) jar pepperoncini peppers and juice
½ cup water
15½-oz. bottle chili sauce
2 T. instant beef bouillon granules or 4 bouillon cubes

Combine soup mix, ketchup, peppers with juice, water, chili sauce and bouillon in crockpot. Add meat and mix well. Cook for at least 6 hours. Stir to separate meat and let cook for an additional hour. Serve on hamburger buns.

Lee Przybylski
Weston, Wisconsin

Marinade for Bear

Juice of 1 lemon
½ cup tarragon wine vinegar
2 onions, sliced
1 tsp. chili powder
½ cup water
2 tsp. salt
2 bay leaves
¼ tsp. black pepper
½ cup ketchup
1 clove garlic, crushed

Mix lemon juice, vinegar, onion, chili powder, water, salt, bay leaves, black pepper, ketchup and garlic. Place bear meat in glass bowl and cover with mixture. Marinate for at least 36 to 48 hours in refrigerator, depending how tough meat is. If desired, cover meat and marinade with ½ cup oil to seal in mixture and keep meat from discoloring.

William Ostermeyer
Kilbourne, Illinois

Roast Wild Boar in Cherry Sauce

3- to 4-lb. wild boar roast
3 to 6 cloves
1 large onion or 6 pearl onions
2 carrots, sliced
2 bay leaves
1 lemon, cut in half
1 cup vegetable or beef broth
Salt
Pepper
⅔ cup grated rye bread
1 tsp. sugar
Pinch of cinnamon
¼ cup butter, melted
8 oz. canned sour cherries
1 slice white bread
8 oz. canned sour cherries

Sear meat on all sides and place in roasting pan. Add clove-studded onion, sliced carrots, bay leaves, broth and half of lemon, sliced. Sprinkle roast with salt and pepper; cover and bake for 2½ hours at 325°F.

Mix grated rye bread, sugar and cinnamon. Brush cooked roast with melted butter and sprinkle with rye bread crumb mixture. Brown under broiler until crusty. In saucepan, cook cherries white bread and zest of remaining lemon half.

Brandon McKinniss
Harker Heights, Texas

Roast Wild Boar in Cherry Sauce

WILD STEW

¼ lb. elk, cut into 1-inch cubes
¼ lb. venison, cut into 1-inch cubes
¼ lb. pheasant, cut into 1-inch cubes
¼ lb. rabbit, cut into 1-inch cubes
Salt
Pepper
2 T. olive oil
2 medium onions, diced
5 carrots, diced
3 potatoes, diced
1 bunch celery, diced
2 turnips, diced
4 cloves garlic, minced
⅛ cup fresh parsley, finely chopped
⅛ cup fresh basil, finely chopped
2 T. fresh thyme, finely chopped
2 T. fresh oregano, finely chopped
1 tsp. fresh sage, finely chopped
2 cups beef stock or game stock (below)
Roux to thicken (below)

ROUX

1 part clarified butter, melted, to 4 to 5 parts flour. Whisk together, adding flour until it reaches a thick, doughy consistency. Add to stocks and sauces to thicken.

STOCK

5 lbs. bones
Salt
Pepper
2 large onions, cut into large chunks
1 head celery, cut into large chunks
1 bunch carrots, cut into large chunks
2 bulbs garlic, cloves separated
Water

Season elk, venison, pheasant and rabbit with salt and pepper. Heat oil in large skillet; sear meat. Add onions, carrots, potatoes, celery and turnips. When vegetables are almost tender, add garlic, parsley, basil, thyme, oregano and sage. Add stock and bring to a boil; reduce heat and simmer for 2 hours. Add roux to thicken. Season with salt and pepper.

Wash bones, season them with salt and pepper and place in large pan. Bake at 375°F for about 1 hour, turning occasionally. Add onions, celery, carrots, garlic; stir. Bake until burned on edges. Transfer all to large stockpot, cover with water, and heat to boiling. Reduce heat and simmer for 4 hours, adding water if necessary. Strain, cover and refrigerate for up to 2 or 3 weeks. Thicken with roux for brown sauce.

Mark Martin
Covington, Ohio

Hot Chili Sauce

Cubed elk steak or ground venison,
   cooked
12 to 14 dried red chile pods
1 to 2 cloves garlic
3 to 4 cups water
1 tsp. salt
1 tsp. sugar or honey

Place chile pods in oven on baking sheet at 350°F to 400°F just until you can smell them. Remove from oven, let cool. Remove stems and seeds. Place in blender with garlic, water, salt and sugar or honey; blend until smooth. Place in pot and heat to boiling, reducing to a thin gravy-like sauce. Serve as a sauce with any cooked game meat or add meat and pinto beans to make chili. This also makes an excellent enchilada sauce.

Don Miller
Flora Vista, New Mexico

Cree Blueberry Pemmican

5 lbs. moose, caribou or deer, sliced
1 qt. blueberries, raspberries or gooseberries,
   mashed until juicy

Marinate meat in crushed fruit overnight in refrigerator. Put in dehydrator or oven (with door open) at 150°F overnight or until strips are leathery. This is a very stable and nutritious trail food used by the Cree Indians of Northern Canada.

James R. Mansell
Callander, Ontario, Canada

Elk Steak Roll-ups

1½ to 2 lbs. boneless elk steaks
¼ cup melted margarine
¼ cup chopped onion
2 cups fresh bread cubes
½ cup chopped celery
½ tsp. poultry seasoning or sage
½ tsp. salt
½ tsp. garlic powder
¼ tsp. pepper
¼ tsp. parsley flakes
1 cup flour
2 to 3 T. vegetable oil
10¾-oz. can cream of mushroom soup
1½ cups water

Flatten meat to ⅓ inch. Cut into 6 to 8 pieces. Combine margarine, onion, bread cubes, celery, poultry seasoning or sage, salt, garlic powder, pepper and parsley flakes; mix well. Put about ⅓ cup of mixture on each piece of meat; roll up and fasten with toothpicks. Roll in flour. Brown in hot oil. Mix soup and water; pour over roll-ups. Cover and simmer for 1½ to 2 hours or until meat is tender. Serve over rice or noodles.

Gary Nelson
Pioche, Nevada

Venison Stir-Fry

VENISON STIR-FRY

1 lb. caribou, deer, elk or moose round steak,
   sliced across grain to ⅛ x 1 x 2 inches
1 T. oyster sauce
3 T. rice wine
3 T. soy sauce
1 T. rice wine or dry sherry
2 T. peanut oil
6 to 8 scallions, sliced, including some green stalk

Mix oyster sauce, 3 tablespoons rice wine, soy sauce, and 1 tablespoon rice wine or sherry. Add meat and let stand for at least 1 hour, stirring occasionally. Heat oil in wok. Drain meat and add to wok. Cook for 3 to 4 minutes or until meat is done. Add scallions and cook for another minute or so. Serve over hot rice.

Gary Shaw
Enumclaw, Washington

PINEAPPLE CHOPS

6 wild pig or sheep chops
⅓ cup salad oil
20-oz. can pineapple chunks
½ cup soy sauce
¼ cup minced onion
1 T. packed brown sugar
1 clove garlic, crushed
1 T. wine vinegar

Brown chops in oil. Drain pineapple, reserving juice; set fruit aside. Mix pineapple juice with soy sauce, onion, brown sugar, garlic and wine vinegar. Reduce heat to low and pour sauce over chops. Simmer until done. Garnish with toasted sesame seeds and serve over rice with reserved pineapple chunks.

Jan Perry
Santa Rosa, California

TENDER BUFFALO SIRLOIN TIP ROAST

4 lbs. buffalo sirloin tip roast
4 cloves garlic, peeled and slivered
Seasoned salt
Freshly ground black pepper

Preheat oven to 325°F. Wipe roast and pat dry. Cut shallow slits in surface of roast and insert slice of garlic in each slit. Generously sprinkle with seasoned salt and pepper. Place roast on rack and cook for 1¼ hours (rare or 140°F), 1½ hours (medium rare or 160°F) or 1¾ hours (well-done or 170°F). Transfer meat to carving board and let stand for 10 minutes. Carve into thin slices and serve.

If you plan to use for sandwiches, cook the day before and chill without slicing. Slice cold meat very thin and place it in buttered crusty rolls. The thinner you slice it the more tender the meat seems.

Gary Shaw
Enumclaw, Washington

STUFFED MOOSE HEART

1 moose or venison heart, cleaned and deveined
1 lb. hamburger
1 onion, chopped
½ cup chopped celery
Sage
Pepper
Garlic
Poultry seasoning
Bacon slices to cover

Mix hamburger, onion, celery, sage, pepper, garlic and poultry seasoning. Stuff heart with mixture. Cover heart with strips of bacon, using toothpicks to hold in place. Bake, covered, for 1½ to 2 hours at 325°F. Serve hot or cold for sandwiches.

James R. Mansell
Callander, Ontario, Canada

Pineapple Chops

BRAISED BUFFALO SHORT RIBS FOR TWO

4 to 8 buffalo short ribs (about 1½ lbs.)
6 T. water
6 T. olive oil, divided
4 tsp. Dijon mustard
4 tsp. red wine vinegar
3 T. fresh basil
3 T. rosemary
3 T. thyme
¼ tsp. freshly ground black pepper
8 oz. canned or fresh tomato sauce

In small bowl, combine water, 2 tablespoons olive oil, mustard, vinegar, basil, rosemary, thyme and pepper; mix well. Place ribs in large resealable plastic bag or shallow glass container. Set aside half of the marinade (about 3 oz.). Pour remaining marinade (about 3 oz.) over ribs; turn to coat. Cover and refrigerate for several hours. Drain; discard marinade. Brown ribs in remaining 4 tablespoons olive oil. Transfer to shallow, greased 1-quart baking dish. Combine tomato sauce and reserved marinade; pour over ribs. Cover and bake at 350°F for 1 hour or until meat is tender, basting occasionally.

Gary Shaw
Enumclaw, Washington

CARIBOU ROUND STEAK

2 lbs. round steak
10-oz. bottle teriyaki sauce
1 medium to large onion, chopped
10¾-oz. can cream of mushroom soup
Carrots, sliced
Green bell pepper, sliced
Celery, sliced
Seasonings of choice (i.e., garlic, pepper, hot ingredients)

Marinate steak in teriyaki sauce for a couple of hours; brown in skillet. Add onion toward end of browning. Add soup and a can of water. Add carrots, green bell pepper, celery, seasonings of choice; simmer for 1 hour. Serve pan gravy over boiled potatoes.

Note: Round steak is a lean, tough cut, but can be choice and tender if properly prepared. Cut fibers somewhat with steak cuber (device used for cubed steaks); this makes marinating easier and will prevent curling while browning.

Frank Scholz
Rancho Palos Verdes, California

Canadian Lynx Stew

2 lbs. lynx meat
4 T. shortening
1 small onion, chopped
1 tsp. salt
¼ tsp. pepper
¼ tsp. summer savory
¼ tsp. oregano
4 potatoes, quartered
4 carrots, diced
½ cup chopped celery
2 T. flour
½ cup cold water
1 tsp. Worcestershire sauce

Wash meat well, pat dry, cut into 2-inch cubes. Melt shortening in heavy pot, add meat and cook until nicely browned. Add onion, salt, pepper, savory and oregano. Cover with cold water; bring to a boil. Reduce heat, cover and simmer for 1½ hours. Add potatoes, carrots and celery; continue cooking for ½ hour or until meat and vegetables are tender. Make a paste of flour and ½ cup water; add to stew, stirring until thickened. Just before serving, add Worcestershire sauce. Serve hot.

Note: The meat of the lynx is white and very tender; it provides excellent eating, especially in late fall and early winter.

Wayne Wright
Surrey, British Columbia, Canada

Elk or Venison Heart

1 elk or venison heart
1 apple, with peeling, cut into chunks
1 T. black peppercorns
1 tsp. whole cloves
1 celery rib, cut into large chunks
1 drop liquid hickory or mesquite smoke
   (optional)

Combine heart, apple, peppercorns, cloves, celery and smoke flavoring in large kettle; add enough water to submerge heart. Bring to a boil; reduce heat; simmer for 1 hour or until tender. Remove heart from liquid; discard liquid and vegetables. Cool meat and cut into ¼-inch slices. Serve with a mixture of sour cream and horseradish.

Kate Hoppe
Powell, Wyoming

Wild Boar Spareribs
with Sauerkraut

1 slab wild boar spareribs
32-oz. jar or packet sauerkraut
3 slices bacon, diced
2 baking apples, cored and sliced
12-oz. bottle beer
Salt
Freshly ground pepper

Drain sauerkraut, wash thoroughly under cold running water and let soak in a pot of water for about 15 minutes; squeeze completely dry. Place on paper towels and set aside. Cover bottom of roasting pan with sauerkraut; top with bacon, apples and beer. Place ribs on top and sprinkle with salt and pepper. Bake for 1½ hours at 350°F or until ribs are tender and meat falls off bones. Baste occasionally with pan juices to keep meat moist.

Gary Shaw
Enumclaw, Washington

Chapter 3

GROUND
VENISON & BIG GAME

No matter how you slice it (as the old saying goes), you'll end up with a lot of ground meat from your deer and other big game animals. The old standbys (chili, meatloaf, burgers, meatballs) are fine, but why not add some twists? That's what you'll find here— plenty of ways to keep things interesting, along with some great new ideas too.

VENISON CABBAGE SOUP
(GERMAN CHILI)

1 lb. ground venison
¾ tsp. garlic powder
¼ tsp. black pepper
¼ tsp. ground red pepper (optional)
Salt
2 tsp. chili powder
1 to 2 cloves garlic, minced
1 celery rib, chopped
2 (16-oz.) cans kidney beans, undrained
½ medium head of cabbage, chopped
28-oz. can chopped tomatoes
28-oz. can water
4 to 5 beef bouillon cubes
1 potato, diced into ¼-inch cubes

Brown venison in Dutch oven. Add garlic powder, black pepper, red pepper, salt, chili powder, garlic, celery, beans, cabbage, tomatoes, water, bouillon and potato. Bring to a boil; reduce heat; cover and simmer for 1½ hours.

Note: If substituting ground beef, drain fat prior to adding other ingredients.

Richard Hite
Williamsburg, Ohio

ELK 'N' KRAUT

1½ lbs. ground elk
2 to 3 T. oil
3 potatoes, diced
1 cup water
2 tsp. salt
1 tsp. pepper
1 egg, beaten
2 T. ketchup, chili sauce or barbecue sauce
32-oz. jar sauerkraut, drained
2 slices wheat bread, diced, or 1 cup croutons
1 onion, chopped
2 T. packed brown sugar
Cheese slices (optional)

Heat oil in 12-inch Dutch oven. Add meat, potatoes, water, salt, pepper, egg, ketchup, sauerkraut, bread, onion and brown sugar. Stir once. Cover and don't peek! Simmer for 1½ hours. If desired, add thin slices of cheese and let sit with lid on for 1 minute until cheese melts.

Note: If cooking over a campfire, be careful not to put too many coals under oven or mixture will stick to bottom of pan.

James Woods Jr.
Boise, Idaho

STOVE-TOP TACO SUPPER

2 lbs. ground venison
2 (16-oz.) cans hot chili beans with juice
2 (19-oz.) cans diced tomatoes and green chiles with juice
11½-oz. can picante vegetable juice
11-oz. can Mexi-corn, drained
2 envelopes taco seasoning

GARNISH OPTIONS
Tortillas
Shredded cheddar cheese
Chopped onion
Shredded lettuce
Taco sauce

Brown meat in Dutch oven; drain. Stir in beans, tomatoes, vegetable juice, corn and taco seasoning. Simmer for 15 to 20 minutes or until heated through. Garnish as desired.

Bob Hainstock
Marquette, Michigan

JOHN'S NORTHWEST CHILI

2 lbs. ground deer, elk, moose or any wild meat
3 oz. tomato paste
4 cups canned or fresh tomatoes, coarsely chopped
5 cups beef broth
1 cup red wine
¼ cup apple cider vinegar
2 tsp. chili powder
2 tsp. cumin
1 tsp. oregano
1 tsp. black pepper
3 T. oil, divided
2 large onions, coarsely chopped
1 head of garlic, minced
4 cups kidney beans, fully cooked
1 green bell pepper, coarsely chopped
1 red bell pepper, coarsely chopped
1 habanero pepper, finely chopped (optional)
1 jalapeño pepper, finely chopped (optional)

In 6-quart slow cooker, combine tomato paste, tomatoes, broth, red wine, vinegar, chili powder, cumin, oregano and black pepper. Bring to a slow boil. In large skillet, heat 1½ tablespoons oil and brown meat. Add to mixture in slow cooker. Add remaining 1½ tablespoons oil to skillet. Add onions, garlic, beans and peppers; cook for 5 minutes to soften. Add to slow cooker. Cover and simmer for at least 2 hours; best if simmered all day. Tastes better second day.

John R. Workman
Auburn, Washington

Venison-Stuffed Mushrooms

VENISON-STUFFED MUSHROOMS

1 lb. ground venison
1 lb. large whole mushrooms
¾ cup finely chopped onion
1 to 2 cloves garlic, chopped or minced
3 T. butter, divided
½ cup red table wine
½ cup juice from jar of jalapeño-stuffed
   olives
½ cup Parmesan cheese, divided
3 cups bread crumbs (from 4 to 5 slices
   bread)
Salt
Pepper

Brown venison; cook only until rare and set aside. Clean mushrooms and remove stems. Remove mushroom centers so they can be stuffed. Finely chop stems. Fry onions, mushroom stems and garlic in butter.

Add venison, ½ cup wine, olive juice, most of Parmesan cheese (save enough to sprinkle over stuffed mushrooms) and bread crumbs. Mix, and stuff mushrooms. Place mushrooms in clean cast-iron skillet in single layer. Sprinkle with remaining Parmesan cheese, salt and pepper. Fill skillet with wine just above bottom of mushrooms. Bake for 20 minutes at 350ºF or until cheese melts. Garnish serving plate with jalapeño-stuffed olives.

Steven Howe
Shakopee, Minnesota

BUFFALO MEATLOAF

8 oz. ground buffalo
1 egg, beaten
¼ cup fresh corn, cut from cob
¼ cup chopped onion
¼ cup seasoned bread crumbs
1 tsp. Dijon mustard
¼ tsp. fresh thyme, chopped
1 to 2 T. ketchup or salsa

Combine egg, corn, onion, bread crumbs, mustard and thyme in bowl. Add meat and mix well. Shape into 5 x 3-inch loaf. Place in ungreased shallow baking pan. Bake uncovered at 350ºF for 15 minutes. Remove from oven and drizzle with ketchup or salsa. Bake for 15 minutes longer or until meat is no longer pink.

Gary Shaw
Enumclaw, Washington

STEVE'S SAUSAGE BALLS

1 lb. venison breakfast sausage
1 cup flour
8-oz. pkg. shredded cheese

Mix flour with sausage; mix well. Add cheese and mix well. Form small balls and place in glass baking dish. Bake at 350ºF for 45 to 60 minutes or until done.

Steve Heck
St. Clairsville, Ohio

BURGER SOUP

1½ to 2 lbs. ground venison or other game meat
6 large carrots, chopped
6 large celery ribs, chopped
3 large green onions, chopped
2 to 3 large fresh tomatoes
1 to 1½ cups barley
46-oz. can vegetable juice
2 (1.4-oz.) pkgs. dried vegetable soup mix
Seasoned salt
Pepper
Water

Brown meat in 10-quart kettle. Add carrots, celery, onions, tomatoes, barley, vegetable juice and soup mix. Season with salt and pepper and add water to cover. Simmer on medium heat until vegetables are tender, stirring frequently to keep from burning. The most important thing about this recipe is to let it cool overnight and reheat it when ready. This helps spices to blend into the mixture for the full benefit.

Jeff Stricker
Anoka, Minnesota

SMOKY MEATLOAF

3 lbs. lean ground venison, beef or turkey
1 cup dried bread crumbs (preferably Panko, Japanese bread crumbs)
2 large eggs, beaten
Salt
Pepper
1 whole garlic head, finely chopped
2 celery ribs, finely chopped
1 large potato, finely shredded
2 whole carrots, finely shredded
1 medium onion, finely chopped
¼ cup ketchup or barbecue sauce
2 T. balsamic vinegar
1 tsp. dill weed
1 tsp. basil leaves
⅓ cup whiskey

Combine bread crumbs, eggs, salt and pepper, garlic, celery, potato, carrots, onion, ketchup or barbecue sauce, vinegar, dill weed, basil and whiskey. Add meat and mix thoroughly. Divide the mixture into 2 or 3 disposable, recyclable, aluminum loaf pans. Put pans in smoker at 300°F to 325°F until internal temperature reaches 160°F. Let stand for 10 minutes before removing from pans.

Rob Wodzinski
Iron River, Michigan

Venison Meatballs in Savory Tomato Sauce with Spaghetti

1½ lbs. ground venison
⅔ cup fine bread crumbs
¼ tsp. garlic powder
2 tsp. chili powder
½ cup milk
¼ cup grated Parmesan cheese
1 egg, beaten
1½ tsp. beef bouillon granules
2 to 3 T. cooking oil

Sauce

½ tsp. onion powder or minced onion
¼ tsp. garlic powder
8-oz. can tomato sauce
6-oz. can tomato paste
1½ cups water
1 tsp. basil
1 T. dried parsley
1 tsp. dried oregano leaves
2 tsp. beef bouillon granules
¼ to ½ tsp. pepper

Combine ground venison, bread crumbs, garlic powder, chili powder, milk, Parmesan cheese, egg and bouillon in a bowl; mix thoroughly. Form walnut-sized meatballs. Heat oil in large, covered skillet and brown meatballs on all sides. Add more oil, if necessary.

Meanwhile, mix sauce: Combine onion powder or minced onion, garlic powder, tomato sauce, tomato paste, water, basil, parsley, oregano, bouillon and pepper in saucepan. Simmer, covered, for 30 minutes. Pour over meatballs and simmer, covered, for about 45 minutes. Stir occasionally.

James Russell York
Louin, Mississippi

Super-Hot Sinus-Cure Chili

4 lbs. ground venison
1 large onion
4 cloves garlic
2 (10-oz.) cans tomatoes with green chiles
28-oz. can stewed tomatoes
1 qt. hot water
1 T. oregano
1 T. cumin
6 heaping tsp. chili powder
1 T. crushed dry chili pepper
1 tsp. cayenne pepper
1 tsp. black pepper
6 T. picante sauce
2 jalapeño peppers, finely chopped
Salt

Mix onion and garlic with meat and brown thoroughly. Crush tomatoes and add to hot water. Add oregano, cumin, chili powder, chili pepper, cayenne pepper, black pepper, picante sauce, jalapeño peppers and salt. Bring to a boil. Reduce heat and simmer for 2 to 2½ hours, stirring occasionally. Serve hot with plenty of crackers.

W. Guy Hilliard
Red Oak, Texas

BARBECUED ELK MEATBALLS

2 lbs. lean ground elk or venison
1 egg
8 to 10 saltine crackers, crushed
⅛ cup barbecue sauce
Cooking oil
⅔ cup ketchup or barbecue sauce
¼ cup packed brown sugar
1 onion, chopped
⅛ cup lemon juice
⅛ cup water
Salt
Pepper
1 tsp. vinegar (optional; use for sweet-and-sour version)
½ tsp. paprika (optional; use for sweet-and-sour version)
Tabasco (optional; use for spicy version)

Mix egg and cracker crumbs with barbecue sauce. Add meat and mix well. Roll into 1-inch balls and brown in hot oil; set aside. Mix ketchup, brown sugar, onion, lemon juice, water, salt and pepper. Add optional ingredients as desired. Place meatballs in 2-inch-deep baking dish with cover. Pour sauce over meatballs and bake for 45 minutes to 1 hour at 325°F.

Note: I usually bake meatballs halfway through the cooking time, then add sauce for the remaining portion of time.

Mark Haase
Kalama, Washington

EASY MICROWAVE CHILI

1 lb. ground venison
1 medium onion, diced
1 green pepper, diced
1 clove garlic, minced
14½-oz. can diced tomatoes
15-oz. can red kidney beans, drained
8-oz. can tomato sauce
2 tsp. chili powder
1 tsp. salt
¼ tsp. oregano

Crumble ground venison into microwave-safe casserole. Cook for 4 to 6 minutes on high or until no pink remains, stirring once. Drain fat, if necessary. Stir in onion, green pepper and garlic. Cook on high for 4 minutes. Stir in tomatoes, beans, tomato sauce, chili powder, salt and oregano. Cover and cook on high for 5 minutes. Remove cover and stir. Cook, uncovered, at 50 percent power for 20 minutes, stirring at least once.

Mark Wilcox
Kingston, Illinois

Rolled Venison Loaf

2 lbs. ground venison
2 eggs, slightly beaten
1 cup dry Italian seasoned bread crumbs, divided
1 tsp. salt, divided
2 cups sliced mushrooms or 10¾-oz. can cream of mushroom soup
¼ cup finely chopped green onions
¼ cup finely chopped celery
¼ cup snipped fresh parsley
2 T. olive oil
1 cup shredded mozzarella cheese
¼ cup grated Romano cheese
1 T. Italian seasoning
⅛ tsp. pepper

In large bowl, mix venison, eggs, ½ cup bread crumbs and ¾ teaspoon salt; set aside.

In 1½-quart bowl, combine mushrooms, green onions, celery, parsley and olive oil. Cover and microwave on high for 2 to 5 minutes. Stir in mozzarella cheese, remaining ½ cup of bread crumbs, Romano cheese, Italian seasoning, remaining ¼ teaspoon of salt and pepper. Set aside.

Pat meatloaf mixture into 15 x 9-inch rectangle on waxed paper. Spread cheese filling evenly over meat. Roll up tightly from short side by lifting paper. Continue to lift and roll until meat is completely rolled up. Cut into 8 equal pieces. Bake for 1½ to 2 hours at 350°F.

Note: Servings can be individually wrapped and frozen for up to 2 months. Filling also works great with rolled rump roast.

Bob Hainstock
Marquette, Michigan

Venison Barbecue

2 lbs. ground venison, elk, antelope—even bear (bear tends to be greasy)
½ cup chopped onion
¼ cup chopped celery
10¾-oz. can tomato soup
2 T. sugar
¼ cup ketchup
1 T. vinegar
1½ tsp. Worcestershire sauce
Salt
Pepper

Brown venison, onion and celery until golden brown; drain off fat. Add soup, sugar, ketchup, vinegar, Worcestershire sauce, salt and pepper. Mix well and simmer for 30 minutes.

Jeff Houck
New Holland, Pennsylvania

CHILI STEW WITH CHEESE GARLIC BISCUITS

2 lbs. ground venison
5 slices bacon
1 onion, chopped
1 green pepper, chopped
1 celery rib, chopped
14-oz. can pizza sauce
2 cups water
15-oz. can tomato sauce
15-oz. can stewed tomatoes
½ tsp. cumin
½ tsp. oregano
½ T. sugar
1½ T. chili powder
1 tsp. garlic salt
½ tsp. cayenne pepper
2 T. spicy spaghetti seasoning
1 T. celery salt
1 T. hot sauce (or to taste)
2 (16-oz.) cans kidney beans
4½-oz. can mushroom slices

CHEESE-GARLIC BISCUITS

2 cups flour
4 tsp. baking powder
2 tsp. sugar
½ tsp. cream of tartar
½ tsp. salt
½ cup shortening
1 T. chopped fresh parsley
½ cup shredded cheddar cheese
⅔ cup milk
¼ cup margarine
¼ tsp. garlic salt

Fry bacon until crisp; remove from pan. Fry onions, pepper and celery with venison in bacon grease until vegetables are soft and meat is browned. Crunch bacon and add to pan with pizza sauce, water, tomato sauce, tomatoes, cumin, oregano, sugar, chili powder, garlic salt, cayenne pepper, spaghetti seasoning, celery salt, hot sauce, beans and mushrooms. Cook on high for 4 to 6 hours—the longer, the better—stirring occasionally. Can be frozen and warmed up later—best if warmed on stove rather than in microwave. Serve with Cheese-Garlic Biscuits (below).

Sift flour, baking powder, sugar, cream of tartar and salt together. Cut in shortening. Stir in parsley and cheese. Add milk, stirring until dough clings together. Drop by spoonfuls onto ungreased baking sheet. Bake for 8 to 10 minutes at 450°F. Melt margarine; stir in garlic salt and brush over biscuits before removing from baking sheet.

Daniel Shumway
Watkins Glen, New York

HUNTER'S HASH

1 to 2 lbs. venison breakfast sausage
5 medium potatoes, diced
4 T. cooking oil
10 to 12 pickled jalapeño peppers (not raw)
Shredded cheese

Brown meat in Dutch oven; drain and let cool. Add potatoes and mix. Pour oil over mixture and set peppers on top of ingredients. Bake at 350°F for 1 hour or until potatoes are done. Remove from oven and sprinkle with shredded cheese; let cool for about 10 minutes. Serve with eggs.

Mike Merrimen
Palmyra, Wisconsin

Chili Stew with Cheese Garlic Biscuits

Venison Meatballs with Sour Cream Dill Gravy

1½ lbs. ground venison
3 slices soft white bread
¼ cup water
2 tsp. salt
¼ tsp. pepper
⅔ cup finely chopped onion
¼ cup butter or margarine
1 T. flour
¾ to 1 cup milk

Sour Cream Dill Gravy
(makes 1½ cups)
2 T. shortening
1 T. flour
½ cup water
1 cup sour cream
¼ tsp. garlic powder
½ tsp. sugar
½ tsp. salt
1 tsp. dill weed

Soak bread in water for 5 minutes. Squeeze out as much water as possible. Combine soaked bread, ground venison, salt, pepper and chopped onion. Blend lightly but thoroughly. Shape into small balls about 1 inch in diameter. Chill for 15 to 20 minutes. Brown in butter on all sides, turning frequently. Cover pan, reduce heat to low and cook for 15 minutes. In small dish, whisk flour into milk; add mixture to pan to create gravy.

Place shortening in skillet. Add flour and brown slowly, blending well. Add water and cook slowly for 3 to 4 minutes. Add sour cream, garlic powder, sugar, salt and dill weed. Heat, stirring until just bubbly. Pour over meatballs to serve or place meatballs in gravy and simmer a few minutes until heated through.

Lawrence Farro
Silver Springs, Florida

Venison-Stuffed Bread

1 lb. ground venison
16-oz. can diced tomatoes, roasted garlic flavor
1 cup ½-inch cubed extra sharp cheddar cheese
¼ tsp. salt
1 tube Pillsbury country bread dough
2 T. melted butter
Grated Parmesan/Romano cheese mix
Monterey steak seasoning

Combine venison, tomatoes, cubed cheese and salt; mix thoroughly. Open dough container and unroll dough into flat sheet. Use rolling pin to thin out and spread dough to 8 x 14 inches. Place venison mixture lengthwise in center of dough. Leave 2 inches at each end and enough room on sides to wrap remaining dough completely over top. After wrapping dough over venison mix, seal both ends of bread roll. Place in baking dish "top seam" side down. Brush with melted butter and sprinkle with grated Parmesan cheese mixture and steak seasoning. Bake for 1 hour at 350°F.

Stephen Gingras
Lowell, Massachusetts

MOOSE CHILI

2 lbs. ground moose
28-oz. can tomatoes
14-oz. jar salsa
14-oz. can pork and beans in tomato sauce
19-oz. can kidney beans
19-oz. can giant lima beans, drained
19-oz. can mixed beans
1 small cooking onion, chopped
1 tsp. chili powder
Salt
Pepper

Brown meat in large kettle; drain. Add tomatoes, salsa, pork and beans, kidney beans, lima beans, mixed beans, onion, chili powder, salt and pepper. Simmer for 1 hour.

Denise Masson
Belle River, Ontario, Canada

TACO SOUP

1 lb. ground venison, elk, moose or caribou
1 medium onion, chopped
½ cup chopped green pepper
15¼-oz. can whole kernel corn with liquid
1 to 2 (16-oz.) cans kidney beans with liquid
14½-oz. can diced tomatoes
8-oz. can tomato sauce
1.25-oz. pkg. taco seasoning

Mix venison, onion, green pepper, corn, beans, tomatoes, tomato sauce and taco seasoning. Simmer over medium heat for 1 to 1½ hours. Serve hot or cold with chips, olives, sour cream or your favorite accompaniment.

Tom Held
Butte, Montana

CAMP STEW

1½ lbs. ground moose, elk or venison
24-oz. can beef stew
15¼-oz. can whole kernel corn, undrained
14½-oz. can green beans, undrained
24-oz. chili con carne with beans
28-oz. can stewed or whole tomatoes, undrained
1 large onion, diced

Cook meat in large pot; drain. Add stew, corn, green beans, chili, tomatoes and onion. Heat, stirring occasionally. Serve with garlic bread.

Kenneth D. Holt
Buhl, Idaho

STUFFED VENISON MEATBALLS

1 lb. ground venison
15 pcs. ½-inch cubed extra sharp cheddar cheese
15 frozen mini-filo dough pastry shells
Honey mustard

Divide venison equally into 15 sections. Place a piece of cheese on each section and roll into a meatball. Place filo pastry in pastry cups on baking sheet. Place 1 stuffed meatball in each pastry shell. Top each meatball with honey mustard. Bake for 1 hour at 350ºF.

Stephen Gingras
Lowell, Massachusetts

Stuffed Venison Meatballs

CANADIAN MOOSE PIE

Pastry dough
1 to 1½ lbs. ground moose meat
8 medium potatoes, sliced
2 onions, chopped
Salt
Pepper
Garlic powder
10¾-oz. can cream of mushroom soup
1 soup can milk
½ cup flour

Layer potatos, onions, meat, salt, pepper and garlic powder alternately in pastry-lined cast-iron pan. Mix soup, milk and flour. Pour over potato and meat layers. Add more milk to fill pan. Cover with top pastry. Bake for 1½ to 2 hours at 325°F. Serve with a salad.

Note: Moose pie can be frozen and reheated later for a quick meal. This is a fourth-generation family favorite.

James R. Mansell
Callander, Ontario, Canada

ELK MEATLOAF

2 lbs. ground elk
½ lb. lean ground pork
1 onion, chopped
3 T. dried parsley
3 T. grated Parmesan cheese
1 tsp. salt
¼ tsp. pepper
½ tsp. oregano
1 cup soft bread crumbs
2 cups milk
2 eggs, slightly beaten
4 slices bacon
1 cup tomato sauce or ketchup

Mix elk and pork with onion. Combine parsley, Parmesan cheese, salt, pepper, oregano, bread crumbs, milk and eggs. Blend into meat mixture. Press into well-greased loaf pan. Overlap bacon strips on top of meat. Bake for 45 minutes at 350°F. Remove bacon slices and pour tomato sauce or ketchup over top. Return to oven and bake for 20 to 30 minutes.

Ray Murley
Oshawa, Ontario, Canada

THE VERY BEST GAME CHILI

2 lbs. ground game meat of choice, fried
    and drained
1 large sweet Spanish onion, chopped
4-oz. can mushrooms or 1 cup chopped
    wild mushrooms
28-oz. can tomatoes
¾ cup ketchup
15-oz. can tomato sauce
15-oz. can brown beans in tomato sauce
2 (15-oz.) cans dark red kidney beans
11-oz. can corn
3 T. chili powder
1 tsp. onion salt
1 tsp. garlic salt
1 T. seasoned salt
1 tsp. pepper
2 T. sugar
1½ tsp. cayenne pepper

Combine fried meat, onion, mushrooms, tomatoes, ketchup, tomato sauce, brown beans, kidney beans, corn, chili powder, onion salt, garlic salt, seasoned salt, pepper, sugar and cayenne pepper in large pot. Simmer for 1 to 2 hours.

Susan Leroux
Peers, Alberta, Canada

VENISON MEATBALLS, SAUERBRATEN STYLE

2 lbs. ground venison
1½ cups soft bread crumbs
2 eggs
3½ cups water, divided
1 tsp. salt
Dash of pepper
4 beef bouillon cubes
⅔ cup packed brown sugar
½ cup raisins
5 tsp. lemon juice
1 cup coarsely ground gingersnaps

Combine venison, bread crumbs, eggs, ½ cup water, salt and pepper; shape into 1½-inch balls; set aside. Mixture will make about 32 meatballs. In large skillet, bring remaining 3 cups of water to a boil; add bouillon cubes, brown sugar, raisins, lemon juice and gingersnaps. Stir until all ingredients are mixed well. Add meatballs and simmer, uncovered, for 20 to 25 minutes. Serve over cooked noodles.

Note: Meatballs can be browned before adding to liquid mixture.

David D. Miller
Harriman, New York

CARIBOU PIZZABURGER PIE

1 lb. ground caribou
1 medium onion, chopped
½ tsp. salt
¼ tsp. pepper
1½ cups milk
¾ cup baking mix
3 eggs
1 cup pizza sauce
1 cup shredded mozzarella cheese

Preheat oven to 400°F. Grease 10-inch pie plate. Brown ground caribou and onion; drain. Add salt and pepper. Spread in pie plate. Beat milk, baking mix and eggs until smooth. Pour over caribou mixture. Bake for 25 minutes at 400°F. Remove from oven and top with pizza sauce, then cheese. Bake for another 5 to 8 minutes.

Erik Holum
Mitchell, South Dakota

CANADIAN WHITETAIL LIVER LOAF
(LIVERWURST)

1 young venison liver, boiled then ground
1½ lbs. ground venison or beef
3 large onions
½ bunch celery
6 eggs
1 bouillon cube
1 cup bread crumbs
1½ tsp. salt
4 T. Worcestershire sauce
Garlic to taste
Bacon drippings

Grind onions and celery; combine with liver and venison. Add eggs, bouillon, bread crumbs, salt, Worcestershire sauce and garlic. Mix well and shape into loaves. Brush tops with bacon drippings. Bake in pan of water at 350°F for 1½ hours. Excellent as main course or sliced for sandwiches.

James R. Mansell
Callander, Ontario, Canada

STUFFED PEPPER SOUP

2 lbs. ground elk or venison
2 qts. water
28-oz. can diced tomatoes with liquid
28-oz. can tomato sauce
2 cups cooked long-grain white rice
2 cups chopped green pepper
2 beef bouillon cubes
¼ cup packed brown sugar
2 tsp. salt
1 tsp. pepper

In saucepan, brown meat; drain. In soup kettle, mix browned meat, water, tomatoes, tomato sauce, rice, green pepper, bouillon, brown sugar, salt and pepper; bring to boil. Reduce heat, cover and simmer for 1 hour or until green pepper is tender.

Mike Merrimen
Palmyra, Wisconsin

VENISON & BEANS

1½ lbs. ground venison, elk or moose
6 slices bacon, chopped
1 medium onion, chopped
16-oz. can pork and beans
16-oz. can hot chili beans
16-oz. can butter beans
⅓ cup packed brown sugar
1½ cups ketchup
2 T. vinegar
1½ T. molasses
1 T. Worcestershire sauce
½ tsp. salt
¼ tsp. prepared mustard

Cook bacon in Dutch oven until crispy. Set aside and remove half of the grease. Brown venison in remaining grease. Add onion, pork and beans, chili beans, butter beans, brown sugar, ketchup, vinegar, molasses, Worcestershire sauce, salt and mustard; mix well. Bake for 45 minutes at 350ºF or put in Crock-Pot and slow cook on low for 2 hours. Do not cook ahead of time and freeze. Beans will disintegrate if frozen.

Eric Jaeger
Middleton, Wisconsin

LOLLEY'S WILD RICE & VENISON SAUSAGE CASSEROLE

½ lb. hot bulk venison sausage, crumbled, fried and drained
1 lb. wild rice, cooked
½ lb. fresh mushrooms, sliced
1 large onion, chopped
1 large green pepper, cut into 1-inch squares
6 ribs of celery, sliced diagonally
10¾-oz. can cream of mushroom soup, undiluted
2 tsp. salt

Prepare rice. Fry sausage, remove from skillet and set aside. In pan drippings, sauté mushrooms, onion, green pepper and celery. Combine rice, sausage, vegetables, soup and salt, folding together thoroughly. Divide mixture into 2 (2-quart) buttered casseroles. Freezes well at this point. Bake, covered, for 30 to 45 minutes at 350ºF or until heated through. If casserole has been frozen, thaw completely, then uncover last half hour of baking time.

Bob Pozner
Minnetonka, Minnesota

Homestead Venison Meatloaf

2 lbs. ground venison
1 cup milk
2 eggs, slightly beaten
3 T. butter, melted
3 T. minced onion
3 T. minced green bell pepper
3 T. minced red bell pepper
2 T. Worcestershire sauce
1 T. Tex-Joy powdered steak seasoning
1 tsp. beef bouillon granules
1 cup Italian-flavored bread crumbs

Mix milk, eggs, butter, onion, green pepper, red pepper, Worcestershire sauce, steak seasoning and bouillon. Add meat and mix well. Fold in bread crumbs; mix well. Form into a loaf and place in baking pan. Cover with foil and refrigerate overnight if possible to meld flavors. Bake for 1½ hours at 350°F. Check for doneness since oven temperatures differ. Do not overbake—this will cause dryness.

Rodney E. Klunk
Hanover, Pennsylvania

Santa Fe Soup

1 lb. ground venison
16-oz. can ranch-style beans
16-oz. can kidney beans
16-oz. can pinto beans
15¼-oz. can whole kernel corn
10-oz. can Ro-Tel tomatoes
14½-oz. can whole tomatoes
1.25-oz. pkg. taco seasoning
1-oz. pkg. ranch dressing mix
½ cup chopped onion
½ cup water

Cook meat until done; drain well. Add ranch beans, kidney beans, pinto beans, corn, Ro-Tel tomatoes, tomatoes, taco seasoning, ranch dressing mix, onion and water; stir. Simmer for 30 minutes.

Kenneth Kvittum
Chouteau, Oklahoma

Buck & Bacon Balls

2 lbs. ground venison
2 eggs
1½ cups stuffing mix
¾ cup ketchup
½ cup warm water
1.4-oz. pkg. dry onion soup mix
1-lb. pkg. sliced bacon
8-oz. can tomato sauce

Mix venison, eggs, stuffing mix, ketchup, water and soup mix in glass bowl. Roll mixture into golf ball-size meatballs and wrap each with ½ strip of bacon. Arrange in baking dish. Pour tomato sauce over meatballs and bake, uncovered, for 1 hour at 350°F or until brown. Serve with ketchup, barbecue sauce or horseradish.

Tim Naylor
Streetsboro, Ohio

BARBECUE

2½ lbs. ground venison
2 medium onions, chopped
1 tsp. salt
½ tsp. pepper
¾ cup ketchup
1 cup tomato juice
1 tsp. Worcestershire sauce
1 tsp. liquid smoke
2 tsp. vinegar
2 tsp. barbecue sauce

Mix venison, onions, salt, pepper, ketchup, tomato juice, Worcestershire sauce, liquid smoke, vinegar and barbecue sauce. Simmer for ½ to 1 hour or until thickened.

Kenneth Myers
New Oxford, Pennsylvania

BIG BOB'S VENISON CHILI

2½ lbs. ground or cubed venison
1½ lbs. Italian hot sausage
2 large red peppers, chopped
2 thick slices Vidalia onion, chopped
1 lb. red kidney beans, soaked overnight in water, drained
2 to 3 fresh tomatoes, cubed
3 T. Cajun seasoning
3 T. Cajun hot sauce
2 T. ground black pepper
1 T. ground red pepper
4 (14½-oz.) cans Italian-style stewed tomatoes
8-oz. can tomato sauce
6-oz. can tomato paste
Salt
Pepper

Loosely fry ground venison or sear cubed venison in olive oil. Loosely fry Italian sausage; drain. Put all meat into Crock-Pot. Add red peppers, onion, beans, tomatoes, Cajun seasoning, Cajun hot sauce, ground black pepper, ground red pepper, stewed tomatoes, tomato sauce and tomato paste. Cover and cook for 5 hours on high. Season with salt and pepper to taste. Serve with hot buttered garlic bread.

Bob Lintner
Saddle Brook, New Jersey

Elk Meatballs in Onion Gravy

ELK MEATBALLS IN ONION GRAVY

2 lbs. ground elk or other venison
½ lb. lean ground pork
6 T. butter, divided
½ cup finely chopped onions
1 tsp. finely chopped garlic
1 cup soft fresh white bread crumbs
1 egg, lightly beaten
¼ cup pine nuts, coarsely chopped
½ cup milk
¼ cup finely chopped fresh parsley
1 T. finely chopped fresh thyme
1 T. salt
¼ tsp. freshly ground black pepper
2 T. vegetable oil
2 cups game stock
2 T. flour
1 large onion, peeled and thinly sliced

Melt 2 tablespoons butter in heavy 10- to 12-inch skillet over moderate heat. Add 1/2 cup onions and garlic, stirring frequently. Cook for 5 minutes or until soft and translucent but not brown. With a rubber spatula, scrape contents of skillet into a deep bowl. Set pan aside. Add elk, pork, bread crumbs, egg, pine nuts, milk, parsley, thyme, salt and pepper to onion-garlic mixture.

Knead vigorously with both hands. Beat mixture with a wooden spoon until it is smooth and fluffy. Shape each meatball using 1 tablespoon of mixture. Melt remaining 4 tablespoons butter with oil in reserved skillet. Brown meatballs 10 to 12 at a time, turning frequently with slotted spatula, and regulate heat so they color richly and evenly without burning. Transfer to a plate as they brown.

Drain fat from skillet and add game stock. Heat to boiling over high heat, scraping brown particles from bottom and sides as it heats. Return all meatballs to skillet with any liquid that has accumulated on plate. Turn meatballs to moisten them evenly. Reduce heat and simmer, partially covered, for 20 minutes or until no trace of pink shows when meatball is pierced with point of knife. Transfer meatballs to heated platter and drape foil over them to keep them warm. Add flour and onion slices to liquid remaining in skillet and, whisking constantly, cook over low heat for 4 to 5 minutes or until sauce is smooth and lightly thickened. Taste for seasoning and pour sauce over meatballs. Serve at once with mashed potatoes or hot noodles.

Gary Shaw
Enumclaw, Washington

VENISON ZIP DIP

2 lbs. ground venison
16-oz. can refried beans
1.25-oz. pkg. taco seasoning
Water
1 cup salsa
2 lbs. Velveeta cheese, cubed
¼ cup milk (optional)
1 to 2 T. ranch dressing (optional)

Brown venison; add beans, taco seasoning and enough water to mix taco seasoning with meat and beans; cook for 15 to 20 minutes. Put in 5-quart Crock-Pot set on high. Add salsa; stir well and add cheese cubes. While cheese is melting, stir in milk, a little at a time. Add enough ranch dressing to mix with all ingredients. Cook for 3 to 4 hours. Serve as a hot dip with your favorite chips.

Note: *Ranch dressing can be omitted during cooking and added to individual bowls as desired.*

Slow cooker directions: *Brown venison; add beans, taco seasoning and enough water to mix taco seasoning with meat and beans. When this has finished cooking, remove from stove and put into slow cooker set on high. Add salsa, cheese and milk to meat mixture. Add ranch dressing. Cook for 3 to 4 hours.*

Bernard Milyo Jr.
APO AE

VENISON BURGER
WITH WILD LEEKS

5 lbs. ground venison
5 tsp. Morton's Tender Quick
2½ tsp. hickory salt
2½ tsp. garlic powder
2½ tsp. whole mustard seed
2½ tsp. coarse pepper
2½ tsp. dill weed
2½ tsp. onion powder
2½ tsp. sweet basil leaves (crushed)
2½ tsp. paprika
2½ tsp. finely chopped wild leeks
2½ tsp. celery salt

Mix ground venison with Tender Quick, hickory salt, garlic powder, mustard seed, pepper, dill weed, onion powder, sweet basil, paprika, leeks and celery salt. Cover tightly and refrigerate for 24 hours. Mix again and refrigerate for another 2 hours. Form into 3 loaves; place loaves on 1 ungreased baking sheet. Bake for 8 hours at 150°F to180°F. Turn once or twice during cooking time. Slice and serve on sandwiches, pizza, in soup, over noodles or rice or in your favorite recipe calling for sausage.

Rob Wodzinski
Iron River, Michigan

Venison Chimichangas

1 lb. ground venison
1 medium onion, chopped
⅓ cup picante sauce
Salt
Pepper
⅔ cup cheddar cheese, shredded
1 pkg. egg roll wrappers
Oil

Brown venison with onions, making sure you cook until venison has a good crumble texture; drain. Add picante sauce, salt and pepper and simmer until juice is gone; this may take some time. Add cheese and stir until mixed well. Place filling into egg roll wrappers, wet edges of wrappers to seal, roll up and fry in hot oil until golden brown. Serve on a bed of shredded lettuce, top with more cheese, sour cream or a spoonful of guacamole.

Jammy Place
Kentwood, Michigan

Ray's Homemade Venison Scrapple

4 to 5 lbs. ground venison
2½ gals. water, divided
2 to 4 (¼-oz.) pkgs. gelatin
2 to 4 beef bouillon cubes
2 tsp. sage
2 heaping tsp. black pepper
1 tsp. salt
¼ tsp. red pepper (optional)
3 to 5 lbs. cornmeal

Boil venison in 1 gallon of water for approximately 2 hours or until well done. Mix with electric mixer to the consistency of mush (soupy). Transfer mix to a large heavy pot (larger than 16 quarts). Add remaining 1½ gallons of water (more for less meaty taste, less for more meaty taste). Stir in gelatin, bouillon, sage, black pepper, salt and red pepper. Cook mixture until spices are blended. Add more spices if needed (I use 1 tablespoon each of sage and pepper).

Note: At this point it should taste spicier than you prefer because the cornmeal will dull the spices. Add cornmeal by the handful while stirring mixture until consistency allows you to "plop" a spoonful into a pan. ***Note:*** *Consistency should be dry enough to pull away from sides of pot (very thick). Form into loaf pans and allow to cool overnight or until set. Slice into meal-sized portions (approximately 1-pound blocks), and freeze until ready to use.*

Ray Stacey
New Castle, Delaware

Spicy Meaty Mac & Cheese

1 lb. ground game meat
1 large sweet onion (prefer Walla Walla), diced
1 to 2 T. Montreal Steak Seasoning
2 (5½-oz.) boxes macaroni and cheese
2 T. (¼ stick) butter
Juice from 16-oz. jar pepperoncini peppers

Brown meat with onion; add steak seasoning as desired. Set aside. Cook macaroni until soft; drain. Stir butter and cheese packets into macaroni. Add juice from peppers to macaroni in place of milk or water. Mix with meat and stir. Garnish with pepperoncini peppers.

Glenn Heisler
Bainbridge Island, Washington

Chapter 4
SMALL GAME

Deer and big game get all the attention when it comes to magazine articles and hunting books. But small game—squirrels and rabbits for the most part—make for equally exciting hunting and incredible eating. Take some time to take a kid out small game hunting, or just get out and do it yourself. Either way you'll have fun … and you'll love the culinary results when you use these recipes.

Rube's Squirrel Italiano

4 squirrels, quartered
8 oz. Italian dressing
4 T. cornstarch

Parboil squirrel for 25 minutes. Combine Italian dressing with cornstarch. Dip squirrel in mixture and place on a greased baking sheet. Bake for 30 minutes at 350°F.

Tim and Jestin Rubelman
Chesaning, Michigan

Roasted, Fried or Stewed Raccoon

1 raccoon
2 pods red pepper
Salt
½ cup flour
¼ tsp. black pepper

Remove pelt from raccoon. Clean meat; remove kernel-shaped glands found in muscles of the armpits and between legs. You will have to cut into meat a little to extract them.

Place meat in large pot and cover with water. Parboil meat with red pepper and salt. Remove from water and put meat in roasting pan. Sprinkle with flour and black pepper. Roast until done.

Fried: Use only a young coon. Cut into small pieces for frying. Soak these in milk for 40 minutes. Remove meat and roll in flour. Season with salt and pepper. Deep fry in fat. Gravy can be made by pouring off most of fat, leaving just enough to cover bottom of pan. Stir in seasoned flour and cook until brown. Add milk and heat through; cook to desired consistency.

Stewed: Cut meat into small pieces and remove all fat. Cover with water and boil until meat is ready to fall from the bone. Add potatoes, onions, cooked rice and any other vegetables you have available. Skim off fat that rises to the top. To thicken, in separate bowl, combine flour or cornstarch with cold water; add to stew and cook to desired consistency.

Wayne Wright
Surrey, British Columbia, Canada

Deep-Fried Squirrel
Rabbit, Waterfowl or Game Birds

3 fox squirrels, cleaned and cut up
Vegetable oil
Water
1 cup flour
2 tsp. paprika
1 tsp. salt
⅓ tsp. pepper
¼ tsp. curry powder
Dash of garlic powder
1 cup buttermilk

Heat oil in deep fryer. Parboil squirrel in water until cooked through. You can inject with seasonings at this time for extra flavorings. Mix flour, paprika, salt, pepper, curry powder and garlic powder. Dip squirrel pieces into buttermilk, then into flour mixture. Gently place pieces into deep fryer for 2 to 3 minutes. Check occasionally with knife. Pieces will be very hot. Serve hot with dumplings or potatoes and vegetables.

Bill Mayhew
Essexville, Michigan

COUNTRY RABBIT SUPPER

1 rabbit, rinsed, dried and cut into serving pieces
16-oz. jar sauerkraut, drained and rinsed at least twice
1½ cups apple cider
1 bay leaf, crumbled
4 to 6 medium red potatoes, scrubbed

Place sauerkraut in medium-sized baking dish with apple cider and bay leaf, mixing well. Bury rabbit in sauerkraut mixture. Place potatoes between the rabbit pieces. Cover with foil and bake for 1½ hours at 325°F or until moist and tender.

Gary Shaw
Enumclaw, Washington

CREAMED SQUIRREL

2 squirrels, cleaned and quartered
½ onion, chopped
Water
½ cup (1 stick) butter or margarine
½ cup flour
3 cups milk
1 cup broth from squirrel
1 tsp. salt

Place squirrel in small roaster pan. Put chopped onion on top and add water to just cover squirrel. Bake for 1½ to 2½ hours at 350°F or until tender. Drain broth from squirrel, reserving 1 cup for gravy.

In 1½-quart pan, melt butter over low heat. Stir in flour. Slowly add milk and broth while stirring constantly with wire whisk. Add salt. Increase heat to medium and cook until thickened. Pour over squirrel. Serve over hash browns, bread or toast.

Don Linse
Maiden Rock, Wisconsin

SQUIRREL DUMPLINGS

3 squirrels, cut up
2 cups flour
1 egg
1 tsp. salt
¾ cup broth
Salt
Pepper

Boil squirrel in 4 quarts of water until tender. Remove squirrel from broth, continuing to boil broth. Let meat cool; remove from bones. Set aside. In large bowl, mix flour, egg and 1 teaspoon salt with broth; roll into ball. Return meat to boiling broth. On floured cutting board, use rolling pin to roll dough ball to 1/16 inch thick. Cut into 1-inch-wide strips; drop strips one at a time into boiling broth. Gently shake pot after last dumpling is added to prevent sticking. Cook for approximately 10 to 15 minutes or until dumplings are tender. Season with salt and pepper.

Chris Patty
Rossville, Georgia

Hot 'n' Spicy Dutch Oven Wild Game

1 large or 2 small rabbits
Salt
Pepper
2 large Vidalia onions, sliced into ¼-inch segments
10 to 20 cherry tomatoes
1-lb. pkg. baby carrots
5 celery ribs, cut into 3-inch lengths
2 green, red or yellow peppers, cut into ½-inch-wide strips
10 fresh jalapeño peppers or 2 habanero chile peppers, whole
4 (12-oz.) cans beer (may substitute water)
2 tsp. chili powder

Season meat with salt and pepper; place in cast-iron Dutch oven. Distribute onions, tomatoes, carrots, celery and peppers evenly around meat. Do not cut open jalapeño peppers or habanero chiles before placing on top. Cover with enough beer or water to a depth of 1 to 2 inches. Sprinkle chili powder over top. Cover with lid and place in campfire, covering top with coals. Replenish liquid if necessary. Meat should fall off bones. Remove from campfire and serve from Dutch oven.

Note: If baking in oven, you may or may not want to cover Dutch oven. For best infusion of game and vegetables, cook covered. Cook for 40 to 50 minutes at 350ºF or until meat is done. If cooking on top of stove, cook for 40 to 50 minutes or until meat is done.

Neil Smith
Winfield, Kansas

Pot-Baked Rabbit

Legs from 6 rabbits, shot pellets removed
1½ cups water
4 medium potatoes, washed and any eyes removed, or 4 cored, peeled, quartered quince
15-oz. can tomato chunks
6-oz. can tomato paste
3 cloves garlic, crushed
1 large onion, diced
Salt
Pepper
4 carrots, cut diagonally to ½-inch pieces
4 celery ribs, cut to ½-inch pieces

Place oven rack about 3 inches above heat source. Preheat oven to 300ºF. Add water to a 9 x 12-inch pan. Place potatoes and rabbit legs in pan. Bake for 20 minutes. Mix tomato chunks, tomato paste, garlic and onions; season with salt and pepper. Set some of mixture aside and brush the rest onto rabbit legs and potatoes. Bake for 10 minutes. Turn legs and potatoes and apply balance of mixture. Add water if necessary. Add carrots and celery and bake until meat is done. Serve with Italian or French bread.

Note: Balance of rabbit can be used for stew.

Vartkess Tarbassian
Framingham, Massachusetts

Hot 'N' Spicy Dutch Oven Wild Game

RABBIT IN BEER

1 rabbit, cut up
12-oz. can beer
¼ cup chopped onion
¼ tsp. nutmeg
¼ tsp. paprika
Salt
Pepper
3 T. butter, melted

Rinse rabbit and place in glass dish or heavy-duty plastic bag. Combine beer, onion, nutmeg, paprika, salt and pepper and pour over rabbit. Marinate for 3 to 4 hours in refrigerator, turning every hour. Remove rabbit pieces from marinade and place on smoker grid. Brush pieces liberally with melted butter. For charcoal, use 5 pounds charcoal, 3 quarts water and 1 to 2 wood sticks; smoke for 1 to 2 hours. If using electric smoker, use 3 quarts hot water and 1 to 2 wood sticks; smoke for 1 to 2 hours.

Don Wallis
Ely, Nevada

SQUIRREL WITH GRAVY

3 black or grey squirrels, skinned, cut up;
   remove loins from backs
1 tsp. salt
2 tsp. pepper
6 to 7 slices bacon (enough to cover squirrels)
Carrots
1 medium onion, chopped

Put about ½ inch of water in roaster; add meat. Season with salt and pepper and place bacon over meat. Surround with carrots and onion. Bake for 1 hour at 450°F. Reduce to 275°F for 1 hour. Remove squirrel, carrots and onion from roaster to make gravy. Add a little more water and season with salt and pepper. Return meat to roaster; return to oven until meat is tender. Serve with mashed potatoes.

Susan Leroux
Peers, Alberta, Canada

SQUIRREL STEW

3 squirrels, cut up
¼ cup plus 3 T. flour, divided
1 tsp. salt
½ tsp. pepper
2 slices bacon
2 T. butter
28-oz. can whole tomatoes
1 onion, chopped
1 heaping T. brown sugar
2 potatoes, cut into ½-inch cubes
10-oz. pkg. frozen lima beans
1 cup frozen corn

Combine ¼ cup of the flour, salt and pepper. Coat squirrel pieces with flour mixture. In Dutch oven, combine bacon and butter over medium heat until butter melts. Add squirrel pieces and brown. Add 5 cups water, tomatoes, onion and brown sugar; bring to a boil. Reduce heat, cover and simmer for 1½ to 2 hours, stirring occasionally. Remove squirrel pieces and let cool. Remove meat from bones. Add meat, potatoes, beans and corn to Dutch oven. Heat to boiling, reduce heat and cover. Simmer until potatoes are tender. Mix remaining 3 tablespoons flour with 3 tablespoons cold water; stir into stew. Heat to boiling. Cook over medium heat, stirring constantly until thickened and bubbly.

Chris Patty
Rossville, Georgia

CREAMED RABBIT

Rabbit, cut up
Flour
Oil
10¾-oz. can cream of chicken, celery or
    mushroom soup
1 soup can water
Salt and pepper

Roll rabbit pieces in flour. Put enough oil in frying pan or Dutch oven to cover bottom; heat. Brown meat in hot oil, then place in roaster. Mix soup, water, salt and pepper and pour over rabbit. Cover with lid and bake for 15 to 20 minutes at 350ºF. Reduce heat and continue baking until tender.

Roger Wakershauser
Portage, Wisconsin

SQUIRREL POT PIE

2 to 3 squirrels, depending on size
2 T. vinegar
Salt
10¾-oz. can cream of mushroom
    soup
1 medium onion, chopped
3 medium potatoes, diced
11-oz. can sweet peas
Pepper
10-count can sourdough biscuits

Place squirrels in cooking pot and cover with water; add vinegar and simmer for 15 minutes. Pour off water; wash squirrels and pot. Return squirrels to pot with fresh water and salt; cook until done. Remove squirrels from pot and reserve liquid. Debone meat and set aside. Add soup to covered skillet or Crock-Pot with 2 soup cans of water; add squirrel broth later as needed. Add onion and potatoes to soup. When potatoes are done, add peas and meat; cook until water boils. Stir and season with salt and pepper to taste. Add biscuits for dumplings. Cook for 10 minutes.

Stephen Wilfong
Harrisonburg, Virginia

BROILED SQUIRREL

2 squirrels
1 tsp. salt
⅛ tsp. pepper
4 T. butter, melted

Skin and clean squirrels. Wash thoroughly and pat dry. Cut in half lengthwise and rub with salt and pepper. Place halves on broiling rack and brush with butter. Broil 6 inches from source of heat for 20 minutes on each side. Baste every few minutes with melted butter and drippings.

Ray Murley
Oshawa, Ontario, Canada

Czechoslovakian Rabbit in Sour Cream Sauce

1 rabbit, cut into pieces
Flour
Shortening or bacon drippings
Dash of salt
Dash of pepper
1 cup sour cream
½ cup milk, half-and-half or table cream
1 cup sliced onion
Caraway seeds (optional)

Roll rabbit in flour. Heat shortening and brown rabbit on both sides. Season with salt and pepper. Place in roaster. Mix sour cream, milk and onion; pour over rabbit. Sprinkle with caraway seeds. Cover and bake for 1½ hours at 325ºF to 350ºF. Check occasionally so it doesn't dry out; add more milk if necessary.

If you want to make gravy, mix 1 tablespoon flour with cold water; add cream mixture from roaster and cook on stove until thickened. Adjust amount of flour according to cream mixture.

John J. Farnik
Buena Park, California

Czechoslovakian Rabbit in Sour Cream Sauce

SQUIRREL SOUP

1 to 2 squirrels, cut into pieces
3 carrots, cut into pieces
2 ribs celery, cut into pieces
1 small onion, chopped
1½ cups wide egg noodles or ½ cup rice, uncooked
¼ lb. smoked sausage, sliced
14-oz. can Italian-style diced tomatoes (seasoned with basil, garlic and oregano)

Boil squirrels in 8 cups water for 1 to 1½ hours or until tender. Add carrots, celery, onion, noodles or rice, sausage and tomatoes. Cook slowly for an additional 30 to 45 minutes.

Patricia Franzina
Mesquite, Texas

SMALL GAME MARINADE

Rabbit, squirrel or animal of choice
1 cup wine
1 cup vinegar
½ cup oil
1 medium onion
3 T. sugar
3 bay leaves
1 T. oregano
1 tsp. nutmeg
2 cups water

Mix wine, vinegar, oil, onion, sugar, bay leaves, oregano, nutmeg and water. Add meat and soak for 3 hours in refrigerator. Can be smoked, if desired.

Dexter Woolcock
Tatamagouche, Nova Scotia, Canada

RABBIT IN BARBECUE SAUCE

3 lbs. rabbit
4 T. flour
½ tsp. salt
¼ tsp. pepper
4 T. cooking oil

BARBECUE SAUCE
2 T. packed brown sugar
1 T. paprika
1 tsp. salt
1 tsp. dry mustard
¼ tsp. chili sauce
A few grains of cayenne pepper
2 T. Worcestershire sauce
1 cup tomato juice
¼ cup chili sauce or ketchup
¼ cup vinegar
½ cup chopped onion

Skin and clean rabbit; wash thoroughly and cut into serving pieces. Dredge rabbit in mixture of flour, salt and pepper. Heat oil in heavy frying pan; brown rabbit on all sides over moderate heat for about 20 minutes. In separate bowl, combine brown sugar, paprika, salt, dry mustard, chili sauce, cayenne pepper, Worcestershire sauce, tomato juice, chili sauce or ketchup, vinegar and onion. Pour sauce over rabbit; cover and bake for 45 minutes at 325°F or until tender. Uncover pan and place under heated broiler, being careful not to let it burn.

Ray Murley
Oshawa, Ontario, Canada

CROCK-POT SQUIRREL

2 to 4 squirrels, cleaned and cut up
2 eggs
1 cup milk
Flour
Cooking oil
2 (12-oz.) jars roasted turkey gravy

Mix eggs and milk. Dip meat into mixture and roll in flour. Fry in hot oil to sear meat on all sides. Place in Crock-Pot. Mix gravy with warm water and pour over squirrel, enough to cover meat; cook for 4 to 6 hours or until tender. Season to taste. Serve with mashed potatoes.

Note: Rabbit can be substituted, but cooking time is twice as long.

Thomas A. Frase
Wadsworth, Ohio

ROAST BEAVER WITH PARSNIPS

1 young beaver (kits or yearlings are best)
Cold water
Vinegar
Salt
3 bay leaves
½ cup melted butter
1 T. lemon juice
1 tsp. Worcestershire sauce
2 large parsnips, sliced into circles
5 medium carrots, sliced length-wise
2 large onions, quartered
4 potatoes, quartered

The best beaver to use is a younger one taken in late fall or winter, but you must be sure to strip away all fat. Soak overnight in cold water and vinegar; if there is some blood in an area of meat, be sure to salt this as well.

Remove from soak and parboil to ensure that all fat is removed.

Place beaver in roasting pan. Add bay leaves. Mix melted butter, lemon juice and Worcestershire sauce; pour over beaver. Cover and bake for 1½ hours at 300°F, basting occasionally. Add parsnips, carrots, onions and potatoes during last 45 minutes to keep them a little crisp. (You may add them earlier if you prefer them stew-like.) The amount of vegetables is determined by preference and the size of your beaver.

Bill Jex
Chilliwack, British Columbia, Canada

HOBO RABBIT

1 whole rabbit, cleaned
Salt
Pepper
10½-oz. can vegetable soup

Season rabbit with salt and pepper. Place in aluminum foil. Pour soup over rabbit. Double wrap tightly. Place in campfire coals or camp oven. Cook for 1 hour and 15 minutes or until done.

John W. Keister
Mifflinburg, Pennsylvania

Bourbon Street Squirrel Legs

BOURBON STREET SQUIRREL LEGS

8 squirrel legs, rinsed in cold
    water
2 T. barbecue sauce
1 tsp. whiskey (I prefer Wild
    Turkey 101)

Mix barbecue sauce and Wild Turkey 101 in plastic container with lid. Add squirrel legs, seal lid and shake to mix well. Refrigerate for at least 2 hours. Grill on medium, turning often, for about 15 minutes, or bake for 30 minutes at 350°F, turning halfway through cook time. For stove-top cooking, peel meat off bone, cover and cook on medium high until done.

John R. Howell
Bath, Pennsylvania

HARE CHARTREUSE

1 rack of hare and hind legs, deboned and cut into
    bite-size pieces
Salt
Pepper
2 T. flour
3 T. oil
Stock or water
1 T. Madeira wine
3 T. butter, divided
Pinch of nutmeg
Salt
Pepper
¼ cup milk
1 egg yolk
4 slices fried bacon, finely chopped
Meat from hare's neck, cooked and finely chopped
Carrots, boiled and sliced
1 parsley or celery root, chopped
2 small cabbages, leaves separated

Season meat with salt and pepper. Roll in flour and brown slightly in hot oil. Add stock or water with wine and simmer until soft. Meanwhile, prepare filling: Mix 1 tablespoon butter, nutmeg, salt, pepper, milk and egg yolk; beat until foamy. Add bacon and meat from neck.

Grease glass casserole with remaining 2 tablespoons butter. Line with carrots and parsley. Cover bottom of pan with filling. Blanch cabbage and wrap around browned meat pieces; place in casserole. Top with additional cabbage leaves. Bake for 1 hour at 350°F.

David Lucero
Los Lunas, New Mexico

RABBIT PIE

2 young rabbits, cut into serving pieces
1 onion, sliced
1 slice bacon, cut into strips
1 tsp. salt
Dash of pepper
Flour
1 box biscuit mix

Place meat in kettle and cover with boiling water. Add onion, bacon, salt and pepper. Cover tightly and simmer until tender. Thicken broth with flour using 2 tablespoons per cup of liquid. Pour over rabbit. Pour into baking dish. Prepare biscuit dough. Turn onto lightly floured board. Pat in ¼-inch-thick sheet. Cut slits to allow steam to escape. Place over rabbit. Bake at 450ºF for 30 minutes.

Robert Fahrnkopf
St. John, North Dakota

MEXICAN-STYLE BEAVER

1 medium beaver, quartered and fat removed
2 to 4 T. flour
Salt
Pepper
Cooking oil
16-oz. can light red kidney beans
16-oz. can dark red kidney beans
2 large onions, diced
1 cup celery, diced
1 qt. tomato juice
28-oz. can diced tomatoes
1 to 2 T. crushed red pepper (optional)
1 tsp. garlic powder
Chile pepper (optional)
Other vegetables (optional)

Parboil beaver in water until meat turns light gray, skimming fat as it boils. Remove from water, cool to touch and cube meat. Coat meat in mixture of flour, salt and pepper. Brown in oil. Place meat, beans, onions, celery, tomato juice, tomatoes, red pepper and garlic powder in slow cooker. Mix well. Cook slowly for 2 to 3 hours.

Mike Petronio
Pittsburgh, Pennsylvania

CREAMED GROUNDHOG, RABBIT, SQUIRREL OR MUSKRAT

1 medium groundhog, quartered, fat removed
4 medium potatoes, quartered
2 large carrots, diced
1 large onion, chopped
1 cup chopped celery
10¾-oz. can cream of mushroom soup
1 soup can milk
Salt
Pepper

Parboil groundhog until meat falls off bone, skimming as it boils. This will clean meat and remove fat. Place meat in baking dish with potatoes, carrots, onion and celery. Mix soup with milk and pour over meat and vegetables. Season with salt and pepper. Cover dish and bake for 1½ hours at 350ºF or until meat falls off bones at touch of fork.

Mike Petronio
Pittsburgh, Pennsylvania

SHERRIED SQUIRREL

4 squirrels, cut up
2 qts. water
1 T. salt
2 tsp. vinegar
⅓ cup flour
1 tsp. salt
⅛ tsp. pepper
2 T. butter or margarine
2 T. vegetable oil
8 oz. fresh whole mushrooms

SHERRY SAUCE
1 cup chicken broth
¼ cup sherry
1 T. Worcestershire sauce
¼ tsp. seasoned salt
2 to 3 drops hot red pepper sauce

In large glass or ceramic bowl, combine squirrel pieces, water, 1 tablespoon salt and vinegar. Cover bowl with plastic wrap and let stand at room temperature for 1 hour. Drain, discarding liquid. Pat squirrel pieces dry; set aside. Heat oven to 350°F. In large resealable plastic bag, combine flour, 1 teaspoon salt and pepper; shake to mix. Add squirrel pieces; shake to coat. Melt butter and oil in large skillet over medium-low heat. Add squirrel pieces and brown on all sides over medium-high heat. Transfer squirrel pieces and drippings to 3-quart casserole. Add mushrooms. In 2-cup measure, combine chicken broth, sherry, Worcestershire sauce, seasoned salt and hot pepper sauce. Pour over squirrel and mushrooms. Cover and bake for 1½ hours or until tender.

Howard Garlock
Milford, Connecticut

EASY MUSKRAT

1 muskrat
1 T. salt
1 qt. water
1 egg yolk
½ c. milk
1 tsp. salt
½ c. flour
4 T. cooking oil

Remove fat, scent glands and white tissue inside each leg. Soak muskrat overnight in mixture of 1 tablespoon salt to 1 quart water. Cut into serving pieces. Parboil for 30 minutes, drain and wipe with a damp cloth. Make smooth batter by beating egg yolk and milk, then adding salt and flour. Heat oil in heavy skillet. Dip meat in batter, then sauté in hot oil until brown. Reduce heat, cover and cook slowly for 1½ hours or until done.

To Roast: Clean and wash muskrat with salt. Put in roasting pan with a little water and roast for about 1 hour.

To Boil: Clean and wash muskrat. Cover with cold water with salt added. Boil for 1 hour or until meat is soft and falls apart easily. Season with hot pepper sauce as desired.

To Fry: Clean and wash muskrat thoroughly, taking fat off. Cut up and dip in flour mixed with salt, pepper and a little water. Deep fry in hot oil until done.

Wayne Wright
Surrey, British Columbia, Canada

Chapter 5

UPLAND BIRDS

A flushing pheasant, quail or grouse is beautiful. Coming to you in the mouth of a good dog you trained, or in your hand as you admire it in the setting sun, the bird is still lovely and exciting. But upland gamebirds create excitement somewhere else too: on the table! Here are some of the finest recipes we've ever seen for preparing these wonderful birds.

FRIED GROUSE & ONIONS

1 grouse, cut into pieces
⅔ cup butter
½ tsp. salt
¼ tsp. pepper
½ cup thinly sliced onions
1 T. flour
1½ cups milk

Skin and draw grouse; cut into serving pieces and soak overnight in a weak solution of salted water. Drain well, then roll each piece in flour. Heat butter in heavy frying pan, season grouse with salt and pepper and sauté until golden brown and tender. As each piece is cooked, remove from frying pan and keep warm in oven. When grouse is done, add sliced onions to fat in pan and cook until translucent. Stir in 1 tablespoon flour and blend well. Add milk and bring to a boil, stirring constantly. Arrange grouse on platter and pour onion sauce over it.

Ray Murley
Oshawa, Ontario, Canada

PHEASANT ENCHILADAS

1 whole pheasant
2 (10¾-oz.) cans cream of chicken soup
2 cans pheasant broth
4-oz. can diced green chiles
16-oz. carton sour cream
1 lb. cheddar cheese, shredded
1 lb. jack cheese, shredded
10 to 15 (10-inch) flour tortillas
Sliced ripe olives

Boil pheasant in water; reserve broth. Debone pheasant. Mix 2 quarts water with soup, broth, green chiles and sour cream to form a sauce; put a small amount in bottom of 9 x 13-inch pan. Place a little pheasant, cheeses and sauce on flour tortillas and roll up. Place each roll on top of sauce in baking dish. Fill as many tortillas as there is pheasant. Pour remaining sauce and cheeses over tortillas. Dot top with sliced ripe olives. Bake for 35 to 40 minutes at 325°F or until heated through.

David L. Stetzel
Montague, California

BIRDS & BEEF

12 doves or 8 quail
2¼-oz. jar dried beef
½ lb. sliced bacon
8 oz. sour cream
10¾-oz. can cream of
  mushroom soup

Rinse dried beef. Layer bottom of baking dish with beef slices. Place birds, breast-side up, on top of beef. Layer bacon strips across top of birds. Bake, uncovered, for 30 minutes at 350°F. Mix sour cream and soup; pour over meats. Bake, uncovered, for additional 25 minutes. Serve over rice. A good red wine complements this dish.

Note: This recipe also works well with pigeons, pheasant or grouse cut into serving pieces.

John Kneece
Leesville, South Carolina

GRILLED DOVES

4 doves, split down back and flat-
    tened, or 8 dove breasts
¼ cup olive oil
2 cloves garlic or shallots, peeled and
    minced
1 T. fresh rosemary, minced
Salt
Freshly ground black pepper

Light a 1- to 2-inch-thick layer of briquettes in a charcoal grill and let the coals burn until white ash appears on the surface.

Mix oil, garlic or shallots, rosemary, salt and pepper; brush on both sides of birds. Grill 4 to 5 inches from heat for 7 to 8 minutes on each side or until doves are medium-rare. Baste several times with the oil mixture.

Gary Shaw
Enumclaw, Washington

WILD RICE PHEASANT SOUP

½ pheasant, cooked and shredded
⅓ cup butter
1 T. minced onion
½ cup flour
4 cups chicken broth, warmed
1 tsp. salt
White pepper
2 cups wild rice, cooked
1 cup half-and-half
2 T. dry white wine
½ cup grated carrot
¼ cup slivered almonds

Melt butter in large pan. Sauté onion. Add flour with whisk. Whisk in broth and cook until slightly thickened. Stir in salt, pepper and rice. Simmer for 5 minutes. Blend in half-and-half and wine. Continue to heat slowly. Add carrots, pheasant and almonds. Heat to serving temperature. Can be refrigerated at this point and reheated but not boiled as cream will curdle.

Bob Pozner
Minnetonka, Minnesota

PARTRIDGE BREASTS

3 to 4 partridge breasts
Pepper
1 T. butter
12-oz. can beer (lager)
1 T. chicken soup mix
1 T. onion soup mix
2 cloves garlic, sliced

Season meat with pepper and brown in butter. Add beer, soup mixes and garlic. Simmer for 45 to 60 minutes. Serve with rice and vegetables.

Thomas O. Jones
Harrington, Quebec, Canada

Partridge Pineapple Stuffing

4 cups dried bread, cut into ½-inch cubes
¾ cup finely chopped celery
¾ cup pineapple wedges
¼ cup chopped green pepper
Pinch of cayenne pepper
1 tsp. paprika
½ tsp. salt
½ cup chopped bacon
¼ cup butter
2 eggs, slightly beaten

Combine bread, celery, pineapple, green pepper, cayenne pepper, paprika and salt. Cook chopped bacon until lightly crisp; add to bread mixture. Melt butter, remove from heat and stir in eggs. Add to bread mixture, tossing lightly.

Ray Murley
Oshawa, Ontario, Canada

Jellied Meatloaf

1 to 2 cups diced cooked game bird or
    venison
¼-oz. envelope unflavored gelatin
¼ cup cold water
1⅔ cups hot chicken or beef broth
Salt
Pepper
1 tsp. grated onion
1½ T. vinegar or lemon juice
¼ cup sliced stuffed green or black olives
1 or 2 hard-boiled eggs, sliced
3 T. finely chopped celery

Soften gelatin in cold water, stirring gently for a few minutes. Add hot broth and stir until completely dissolved. Add salt, pepper, onion and vinegar or lemon juice. Pour layer of gelatin mixture ¼ inch deep in bottom of sprayed loaf pan or gelatin mold. Let remainder of gelatin mixture thicken, but do not allow it to set. Press some of olives and egg into gelatin in bottom of pan. Add meat, celery and remainder of olives and egg to thickened gelatin/broth mixture. Mix and pour carefully over sliced olives and egg in pan. Chill until firm. Warm pan bottom in hot water. Unmold, slice and serve.

Tom Held
Butte, Montana

QUICK & EASY BREAST OF PHEASANT

2 to 4 pheasant breasts, skinned and
    washed
½ cup water
Salt and pepper
Garlic powder

Place pheasant breasts in glass baking dish. Add water. Sprinkle with salt, pepper and garlic powder. Cover and bake for 1 hour at 300°F or until done. Makes its own gravy. Serve with rice.

Rev. Glover Roston Sr.
Cleveland, Ohio

DOVE, PHEASANT OR DUCK

1 dove, pheasant or duck
1 to 2 (10¾-oz.) cans cream of mushroom soup
1 T. seasoned salt
½ cup whiskey
Whole bread chunks

Place bird in baking pan. Mix soup, seasoned salt, whiskey and bread chunks; stuff bird. Pour any extra over top of bird and bake for 1½ to 2 hours at 350°F. Serve with rice and lemon slices.

Greg Riggs
Pleasant Grove, Utah

CROCK-POT DOVE

8 to 10 doves
Salt
6-oz. can lemonade concentrate
3 T. packed brown sugar
3 T. ketchup
1 T. vinegar

Salt birds. Place breast side up in Crock-Pot. In small bowl, mix lemonade concentrate, brown sugar, ketchup and vinegar. Pour over birds. Cover and cook on lowest setting for 6 to 7 hours.

Note: This recipe also works well with pigeon or quail.

John Kneece
Leesville, South Carolina

Moroccan Sage Grouse & Rice

3 to 3½ lbs. sage grouse or pheasant, cut up
1 T. paprika
2 tsp. cumin
½ tsp. salt
½ tsp. turmeric
½ tsp. ginger
2 cloves garlic, finely chopped
⅓ cup flour
½ cup chicken broth
¼ cup lemon juice
½ cup kalamata or Greek olives
¼ cup chopped fresh cilantro
1 T. grated lemon peel
6 cups hot cooked rice or couscous

Mix paprika, cumin, salt, turmeric, ginger and garlic thoroughly; rub on all sides of grouse. Coat grouse with flour and place in ungreased 13 x 9 x 2-inch baking dish. Mix broth with lemon juice; pour over grouse. Add olives. Bake uncovered for 1 hour at 350ºF or until grouse is no longer pink when center's thickest pieces are cut. Spoon juices over grouse occasionally during baking. Stir cilantro and lemon peel into hot rice or couscous; serve with grouse.

Robert C. Shenk
Paterson, New Jersey

Rosemary Grouse Stew

3 to 4 boneless grouse breasts, cut into bite-size pieces
Oil
¾ tsp. salt
½ tsp. pepper
2 carrots, diced
2 parsnips, diced
1 cup mushrooms, sliced
1 red or green pepper, diced
1 rib celery, diced
1 onion, chopped
2 cloves garlic, minced
¼ cup flour
1 tsp. rosemary
1 tsp. marjoram
1½ cups chicken broth
¾ cup milk
1 T. lemon juice

Heat oil on medium-high heat. Combine salt and pepper and sprinkle over meat. Brown in oil; remove meat and set aside. In same skillet, sauté carrots, parsnips, mushrooms, peppers, celery, onion and garlic until soft. Combine flour, rosemary and marjoram and sprinkle over vegetables. Cook, stirring until flour is absorbed and browned. Add broth, milk and meat and stir. Cover, reduce heat to medium low and simmer for 30 minutes, stirring occasionally. Stir in lemon juice and remove from heat. Serve with hot biscuits.

Note: Chicken may be substituted for grouse.

Colin Ross
Kinuso, Alberta, Canada

Moroccan Sage Grouse & Rice

Smothered Pheasant in Mushroom Sauce

1 pheasant, cut into serving pieces
1/4 cup flour
1 tsp. garlic salt
Freshly ground pepper
2 T. butter
2 T. oil
4 oz. fresh mushrooms, sliced
10 3/4-oz. can cream of mushroom soup

Mix flour, garlic salt and pepper. Roll pheasant in flour mixture until well coated; shake off excess. Heat butter and oil in ovenproof pan; sauté pheasant until richly browned on all sides. Remove meat from pan. In same pan, sauté mushrooms for 3 to 5 minutes or until soft. Pour in soup and stir until well mixed. Return pheasant to pan, turning pieces to coat evenly. Cover and bake at 325°F for 30 minutes or until tender. Remove pheasant pieces to heated platter. Pour mushroom gravy over pieces and serve.

Gary Shaw
Enumclaw, Washington

Pheasant Stew

1 pheasant
2 bay leaves
Salt
2 cups water
2 or more T. shortening
Flour
Pepper

Put pheasant in pressure cooker. Add bay leaves, salt and water. Cook for about 45 minutes. Let cool. Cut meat off bones and into bite-size pieces. Melt shortening in skillet; add meat. Sprinkle with flour. Turn several times to brown on all sides. Add water to make gravy. Add more salt and pepper to taste. Serve over mashed potatoes.

Note: If you do not have a pressure cooker, pheasant can be prepared by simmering in a kettle until tender.

Michael and Kimberly Zion
Julesburg, Colorado

Turkey & Wild Rice Hot Dish

2 to 3 lbs. turkey, cut into 3/4-inch cubes
10 3/4-oz. can cream of chicken soup
1 soup can water
4-oz. can sliced mushrooms
4.3-oz. box Uncle Ben's wild rice and seasonings
1/3 cup uncooked wild rice
1/4 tsp. onion powder

In baking pan, mix meat, soup, water, mushrooms, rices and onion powder. Cover with foil and bake for 1 1/2 hours at 350°F.

Bill Thrune
Dakota, Minnesota

WILD BIRD CASSEROLE

10 to 12 quail or doves
½ cup flour
1 T. salt
1 tsp. pepper
Oil
4.3-oz. box long-grain and wild rice
10¾-oz. can cream of mushroom soup
4-oz. can chopped mushrooms
16-oz. can mixed Chinese vegetables, drained
1 cup water
Salt
Pepper

Mix flour, 1 tablespoon salt and 1 teaspoon pepper. Dredge birds or shake in bag containing flour mixture; remove excess flour from birds so they are lightly coated. Heat oil in nonstick skillet and lightly brown birds. Set aside on paper towels.

Mix rice, soup, mushrooms, vegetables, water, salt and pepper; pour into lightly buttered 11 x 9 x 2-inch ovenproof baking dish. Place birds on top of mixture and bake for 35 to 40 minutes at 350°F or until rice is tender and all liquid is absorbed.

Roy Selby
Greenville, North Carolina

TURKEY FINGERS

Uncooked turkey breast
2 eggs, beaten
Italian bread crumbs
Vegetable oil

Cut turkey breast with grain into finger-size pieces. Dip in egg and dredge in bread crumbs. Cook until golden brown in deep fryer or electric frying pan filled ½ inch deep with vegetable oil.

Philip Stewart
Liverpool, New York

One Awesome Pasta & Wild Game Salad

One Awesome Pasta & Wild Game Salad

1½ lbs. quail, pheasant, elk, venison, boar, etc., freshly grilled, diced, deboned and chilled
3 to 4 T. salt
⅔ cup extra virgin olive oil
2 lbs. Prince or Mueller's Spaghetti (long, regular thickness)
1 large Vidalia onion, diced or chopped
3 medium cucumbers, diced or chopped
4 large or 6 to 8 medium Beefsteak/Big Boy-type tomatoes, sliced into thin wedges, divided
8 oz. grated Romano cheese (use a good Romano or Romano/Parmesan mix; Parmesan is a poor second choice — freshly grated, if possible)
1 large green bell pepper, thinly sliced (optional)
1 large red bell pepper, thinly sliced (optional)
2 (16-oz.) bottles Zesty Italian Salad Dressing

Fill large saucepan ¾ full of cold water and bring to a boil. Add salt and olive oil; stir. Add spaghetti, stirring occasionally to coat pasta with oil.

Meanwhile, combine onion, cucumbers, ¾ tomatoes and Romano cheese in large mixing bowl. Mix thoroughly by hand. It will look like a lot of cheese. If you like green and red bell pepper, add 1 each.

When pasta is fully cooked, not al dente, drain it in collander and rinse with cold water for approximately 3 minutes or until cool. Shake lightly to remove residual water.

Add layer of pasta in large mixing bowl and add vegetable mixture. Add some of the wild game and gently stir with your hands. Repeat with another layer of pasta, vegetables and wild game until you have mixed everything thoroughly and you have a full bowl.

Refrigerate for several hours. When chilled thoroughly, add salad dressing over top and let it flow down through the salad. It is ready to eat, but may be refrigerated overnight. It is better the next day. Top with remaining tomatoes.

Note: Cooking this recipe takes 1 to 1½ hours if meat has already been prepared. Best if marinated overnight.

Gary Johnson
Shelby Township, Michigan

CHOW MEIN HOTDISH

1 lb. shredded duck, goose or pheasant
1 onion, chopped
1 cup chopped celery
1 cup uncooked rice
2 cups water
10¾-oz. can cream of mushroom soup
10¾-oz. can chicken and rice soup
4 to 5 T. soy sauce
2 to 3 T. Worcestershire sauce

Mix onion, celery, rice, water, soups, soy sauce and Worcestershire sauce; add meat. Mixture will be watery. Bake in roasting pan for 1 hour at 350°F. Remove from oven and sprinkle with chow mein noodles. Bake for another 15 minutes. Serve over chow mein noodles.

Richard and Melissa Schirmer
Valley City, North Dakota

WILD RICE SOUP
WITH CHUKAR, QUAIL, GROUSE, PHEASANT OR TURKEY

Leftover bird carcasses
2 cups wild bird stock
1 cup washed and cooked wild rice
1 diced and sautéed onion
2 celery ribs, thinly sliced and sautéed
1 clove garlic, crushed, diced and sautéed
1 lb. Velveeta cheese, cut into cubes
10¾-oz. can cream of mushroom soup
Salt (optional)

Cook leftover bird overnight in Crock-Pot with just enough water to cover. This will create a stock and loosen meat from bones. The next morning, remove bird from liquid with slotted spoon. Cool and separate all meat from bone and check stock for bones. If stock measures more than 2 cups, put into separate pot and boil down. Combine 2 cups stock with meat, rice, onion, celery, garlic, cheese, soup and salt in Crock-Pot. Cook on low for 3 hours or until cheese melts and all flavors have blended. Check and stir often so mixture does not burn. Serve with fresh crusty bread and butter.

JoAnn Hana Walz
Yerington, Nevada

HONEY-BAKED PHEASANT

1 large pheasant, cut up
4 T. (½ stick) butter or margarine
½ cup honey
¼ cup prepared mustard
1 tsp. salt
1 tsp. curry powder

Wash pheasant pieces and pat dry. Remove skin, if desired. Melt butter or margarine in baking pan. Stir in honey, mustard, salt and curry powder. Roll pheasant in mixture to coat all sides and arrange meaty side up in a single layer. Bake for 1 hour at 375°F or until tender and nicely glazed.

Arthur Hamilton
Jaffrey, New Hampshire

PARTRIDGE OR GROUSE FINGERS

Breast meat from 1 bird, cut into thin strips
1 cup flour
1 T. coarse pepper
1 tsp. salt
Dash of onion powder
Dash of garlic powder
2 large eggs, slightly beaten
Cooking oil for deep frying

VARIATIONS OF FLOUR MIXTURE
CAN BE MADE BY ADDING ONE OF
THE FOLLOWING:
1 T. chili powder
1 T. wild game seasoning
1 T. Cajun spice

Combine flour, pepper, salt, onion powder and garlic powder. Dip meat into egg, then flour mixture, repeating so each piece is coated twice. Deep fry for 5 to 7 minutes or until golden brown. Serve with your favorite dipping sauce or hot sauce.

Lorraine Whalen
Thunder Bay, Ontario, Canada

RINGNECK PHEASANT

3 lbs. pheasant
2 T. baking soda
9 oz. beer or 2 jiggers whiskey
Oil
6 T. soy sauce
3 T. raw sugar (brown)
4-oz. can button mushrooms
6-oz. can bamboo shoots
1 cup burdock root (gobo) (optional)
7¾-oz. pkg. cellophane noodles (optional)
Firm tofu
1 large onion, diced
2 green onions, cut into 1-inch pieces

Soak pheasant in baking soda, beer and 7 cups water for 1 hour; rinse and chop into bite-size pieces. Heat oil in large skillet; sauté pheasant for 5 minutes. Combine ½ cup water, soy sauce and sugar; add to pheasant and cook until pheasant is done. Add mushrooms, bamboo shoots and burdock root. Cook for 5 minutes. Add cellophane noodles and tofu. Stir gently so tofu remains firm. Add diced onion; cook for 2 minutes. Add green onion and stir. Serve over hot rice.

Harvey Feuella
Haliimaile, Maui, Hawaii

Roast Pheasant

1 young pheasant
Salt
1 bay leaf
3 to 4 celery leaves
4 slices bacon
⅓ cup salad oil
½ cup mushroom pieces
1 large onion, sliced

Thoroughly salt pheasant inside and out; fill cavity with bay leaf and celery leaves. Wrap pheasant breast with bacon; secure in place with string. Place pheasant in roaster. Pour salad oil over pheasant. Add mushroom pieces and onion slices. Bake for 1½ hours at 350°F. Turn at 30-minute intervals, basting with drippings from pan. Place on platter; remove string, celery leaves and bay leaf. Garnish with parsley and sliced apples.

Michael and Kimberly Zion
Julesburg, Colorado

Partridges in Red Wine

2 (1-lb.) partridges
3 T. flour
½ tsp. salt
2 T. butter or margarine
1 cup beef broth
2 T. finely chopped onion
½ cup burgundy or claret

Split birds in half lengthwise. Combine flour and salt; coat birds with mixture. Brown birds slowly in butter. Add broth and onion. Cook, covered, over low heat for 45 to 55 minutes or until tender. Move to serving platter and keep warm. Skim fat from pan drippings. Stir wine into drippings. Boil vigorously over high heat for 18 to 20 minutes to reduce liquid to ½ cup. Spoon sauce over birds.

Dana Gould
Etna, Maine

Birdman's Wild Game with Port Wine Sauce

6 chukkar breasts and 6 legs, boned and skinned or 6 venison steaks
Flour
Salt
Pepper
2 T. olive oil
½ cup butter
2 shallot cloves, chopped
¾ cup port wine
2 cups beef broth

Tenderize meat by pounding with mallet. Roll meat in flour seasoned with salt and pepper. Heat olive oil and butter in heavy skillet; brown meat and remove to platter. Add shallots to pan for 30 seconds. Add wine and deglaze skillet by scraping bottom; cook for 2 minutes. Add beef broth and heat for 1 minute; add meat and simmer for 20 minutes or until sauce is desired thickness. Additional seasoned flour may be added if sauce is too thin or beef broth if sauce is too thick.

Al "Birdie" Panella
Reno, Nevada

Roast Pheasant

PHEASANT WITH GRAVY

4 to 6 pheasant breast fillets
Flour
Butter
Lemon pepper
Whipping cream

Roll fillets in flour. Brown in butter. Coat generously with lemon pepper. Add enough whipping cream to cover; simmer for 1 to 2 hours. Cream will thicken as it simmers. Serve over wild rice or mashed potatoes.

Jack Lyons
Somerset, Wisconsin

WILD TURKEY SPREAD

2 cups ground wild turkey, cooked
¼ cup chopped walnuts
¼ cup snipped parsley
2 T. finely chopped green onion with tops
2 tsp. lemon juice
1 tsp. Worcestershire sauce
¾ to 1 cup mayonnaise

In mixing bowl, combine turkey, nuts, parsley, onion, lemon juice and Worcestershire sauce. Blend in mayonnaise until desired consistency. Cover and chill. Makes 2 cups. Serve with crackers.

Dana Gould
Etna, Maine

PHEASANT À LA STEVE

4 pheasant breasts
4 slices Swiss cheese
10¾-oz. can cream of chicken soup
½ soup can milk
½ cup sherry (optional)
2 cups herb-seasoned stuffing
½ cup (1 stick) butter

Place breasts in glass baking pan. Cover with Swiss cheese. Mix soup, milk and sherry; pour over cheese. Add stuffing and drizzle melted butter over top. Bake for 45 minutes, uncovered, at 350°F.

Steve Heck
St. Clairsville, Ohio

PHEASANT TENDERS

4 boneless pheasant breasts, cut in half
2 cups Frying Magic
1 tsp. salt
1 tsp. black pepper
1 tsp. paprika
1 cup milk
½ cup olive oil

Prepare seasoned coating: Combine Frying Magic, salt, pepper and paprika in freezer storage bag; mix thoroughly. Cut pheasant halves into small strips. Dip into milk, then drop into coating mix; shake until pieces are coated.

Heat olive oil in frying pan; add pheasant. Cook for approximately 10 to 15 minutes or until done. Serve with French fries or onion rings, or dip into ranch dressing.

Rob Lombardo
Plainfield, Illinois

LEMON PARTRIDGE

4 whole partridge breasts, deboned and
    cut into bite-size pieces
½ cup cornstarch
½ tsp. salt
⅛ tsp. pepper
4 eggs, beaten
3 cups vegetable oil
4 green onions, sliced

LEMON SAUCE
½ cup lemon juice
6 T. packed brown sugar
3 T. cornstarch
4 T. honey
3 tsp. chicken bouillon granules
Zest of 1 lemon

Combine ½ cup cornstarch, salt and pepper in bowl. Gradually blend in ¼ cup water and eggs. In wok, heat oil to 375°F. Dip breasts in cornstarch mixture and fry 2 or 3 pieces at a time for about 5 minutes or until golden brown. Drain on paper towel and keep warm while cooking remaining pieces. In saucepan, combine 1½ cups water with lemon juice, brown sugar, 3 tablespoons cornstarch, honey, bouillon and lemon zest. Cook over medium heat, stirring constantly until sauce boils and thickens. Arrange meat on serving platter. Sprinkle with green onions and pour sauce on top. Serve on a bed of rice.

Note: *This Chinese dish can be prepared with any mild wild game or domestic meat.*

James R. Mansell
Callander, Ontario, Canada

Aunt LaDean's Baked Pheasant

1 average-size pheasant
1 T. salt
Flour
Seasoned salt
Pepper
Shortening
1 onion, cut into 1½- to
   2-inch slices
2 celery ribs, sliced
   (optional)

Cut bird into serving pieces as you would chicken. Mix salt with enough water to cover pheasant; refrigerate for 2 hours. Remove meat from salt water; drain. Coat each piece with mixture of flour, seasoned salt and pepper. Pour ¼ inch shortening in heavy frying pan. Brown meat on all sides until golden brown, adding oil as needed. As pieces brown, place them in roasting dish or baking pan. When all meat has been placed in roasting pan, spread onion slices and celery evenly over the top. Add 1½ to 2 cups water. Cover with foil and bake for 2½ hours at 350°F or until tender. (Older birds will take longer and ovens vary in heating.) Remove cover 15 minutes before meat is done.

LaDean Loften
Submitted by Jim Loften
Albany, Wisconsin

Partridge Baked in Sherry

2 partridges
4 T. butter
1 small clove garlic, chopped
1 small onion, halved
1 T. finely chopped celery
1 tsp. salt
¼ tsp. pepper
½ cup sherry

Remove breasts and thighs from 2 medium-size partridges; wash thoroughly and pat dry. Melt butter in heavy frying pan; add partridge, garlic and onion; cook until partridge is slightly browned. Turn into roasting pan. Add celery, salt, pepper and sherry. Cover and bake for 1½ hours at 350°F or until tender, basting frequently with pan juices to prevent dryness.

Ray Murley
Oshawa, Ontario, Canada

Pheasant with Port Wine Sauce

2 pheasants, cleaned
2 T. melted butter
¼ tsp. salt
¼ tsp. pepper
¼ tsp. onion powder
¼ tsp. dried whole thyme
¼ tsp. nutmeg
¼ tsp. dried parsley flakes
2 slices bacon
¼ cup chicken broth
¼ cup port wine

Port Wine Sauce

½ cup red currant jelly
½ cup port wine
¼ cup ketchup
1½ tsp. cornstarch
½ tsp. Worcestershire sauce

Brush pheasant with melted butter, place breast-side up in large roasting pan on rack and broil for 5 minutes. Mix salt, pepper, onion powder, thyme, nutmeg and parsley; divide equally and rub on birds. Place slice of bacon lengthwise on each pheasant. Insert meat thermometer in breast or thigh (do not touch bone). Cover birds and bake for 1 hour at 375°F. Combine broth and ¼ cup port wine. Remove bacon from birds and baste with broth mixture. Cook, uncovered, for 30 to 45 minutes or until meat thermometer reaches 185°F. Serve with Port Wine Sauce (below).

While birds are baking, mix currant jelly, ½ cup port wine, ketchup, cornstarch and Worcestershire sauce in saucepan, stirring until cornstarch dissolves. Bring to a boil, stirring constantly; cook for 1 minute.

Jim Matousek
Herkimer, New York

Golden Pheasant Nuggets

2 whole pheasant breasts, cut into 1-inch cubes
2 eggs, beaten
1 cup beer
1½ tsp. salt
4 tsp. sesame seeds
1 cup flour

Mix eggs, beer, salt, sesame seeds and flour. Dip pheasant cubes in batter. Deep fry for 3 to 5 minutes at 375°F.

Chris Patty
Rossville, Georgia

HBARR's Smoked Wild Turkey Cheese Ball

1 cup smoked wild turkey
8-oz. pkg. cream cheese
3 T. mayonnaise
½ cup chopped pecans
2 T. chopped parsley

In food processor, blend turkey, cream cheese and mayonnaise. Chill for several hours. Shape into one or two balls. Roll in pecans and parsley. Can be wrapped tightly and frozen for later use or refrigerated for use later that day. Serve with crackers.

Tom and Stacy Quake
Three Rivers, Michigan

Chukkar Stir-Fry

CHUKKAR STIR-FRY

4 chukkar, boned, cubed or sectioned
2 red bell peppers, diced
2 yellow bell peppers, diced
2 green bell peppers, diced
1 large onion, diced
1 bunch broccoli, cut into florets
1 head cauliflower, cut into florets
6 carrots, julienned
3 cloves garlic, minced
4 T. minced gingerroot
4 green onions, cut 1 inch long on bias
1 bunch bok choy, cabbage or Swiss chard, cut
   into 1-inch slices
1 T. hoisin sauce
½ cup soy sauce
¼ cup red wine
2 T. hot chili paste (optional)
Salt
Pepper
Sesame oil

Sauté chukkar in hot skillet. Add bell peppers, onion, broccoli, cauliflower, carrots, garlic, gingerroot, green onions and bok choy, stirring quickly. Add hoisin sauce, soy sauce and wine. Add hot chili paste, if desired. Season with salt and pepper. Add sesame oil last.

Mark Martin
Covington, Ohio

WOODCOCK IN CHABLIS

6 to 8 woodcock breasts and legs, skinned
3 T. butter or margarine
1 medium onion, thinly sliced
1 cup fresh mushrooms, sliced
1 cup chicken broth
½ cup chablis or other dry white wine
3 T. flour
½ tsp. salt
Dash of pepper

Bone breasts. Trim all fat and discard fat and bones. In medium skillet, melt butter over medium heat. Add woodcock legs and breast halves. Cook until meat has just lost its color. Remove from skillet with slotted spoon; set aside. Cook and stir onion in skillet over medium heat for 4 minutes. Add mushrooms. Cook and stir for 2 to 3 minutes or until vegetables are tender. Return woodcock to skillet. In small bowl, blend broth, wine, flour, salt and pepper. Pour over meat and vegetables. Heat until bubbly, stirring constantly. Reduce heat; cover and simmer for 10 minutes or until meat is tender, stirring once.

Blain Oksanen
Antioch, California

"GRILLED" TURKEY

10 to 15-lb. turkey
Items needed:
    10-gal. new galvanized garbage can
    2 x 2-inch wooden stake about 2 ft. long
    10 lbs. charcoal
    Shovel
    Hammer
    Heavy-duty aluminum foil

Light all charcoal in pile and let burn for about 20 minutes or until white. While coals are heating, drive stake into ground, leaving 12 inches above ground. Wrap stake with foil, then spread additional foil on ground around stake to make an area a little bigger than the mouth of the trash can. Place turkey on stake with neck down. Invert garbage can over bird, making sure it does not touch bird. Shovel coals on top of can and around sides. Let cook for 90 minutes undisturbed, then check to see if it is done. If not, place garbage can back on, return coals to top, and check in 15 to 20 minutes.

Merlyn Sisco
Pekin, Illinois

SKILLET PHEASANT

1 or 2 pheasants, cut up (2½ to 3 lbs.)
½ to 1 cup flour
1 tsp. paprika
½ tsp. pepper
1 tsp. salt
4 T. butter
4 medium potatoes, peeled and quartered
4 carrots, peeled and cut into strips
4 small onions, quartered
10¾-oz. can cream of chicken soup
1 cup sour cream and chives topping

Combine flour, paprika, pepper and salt in a bag. Add pheasant pieces one at a time to coat. Heat butter in skillet and brown pheasant pieces. Add potatoes, carrots and onions. Mix soup and topping; pour into skillet. Simmer for 1 hour or until pheasant and vegetables are tender.

Jack Pogge
Kanawha, Iowa

PHEASANT NOODLES

1 large or 2 small whole pheasants
6 chicken bouillon cubes
2 to 3 carrots, chopped
2 tsp. onion powder
2 tsp. celery salt
3 T. parsley
Salt and pepper
1½ (12-oz.) bags egg noodles

Thaw and wash pheasant. Put pheasant in pot with water not quite covering. Add bouillon, carrots, onion powder, celery salt, parsley, salt and pepper. Bring to a low boil and cook for about 1 hour. Remove pheasant and let cool. Remove meat from bones and add to broth. Return to a boil and add noodles. Simmer, uncovered, stirring occasionally or until broth thickens. Add a mixture of flour and water to thicken, if desired.

Tim Rudolphi
Hawthorne Woods, Illinois

TURKEY CHOW MEIN

2 cups cooked, cubed meat
1 cup chopped onion
½ cup chopped green bell pepper
½ cup cooked mushrooms
2 T. butter or margarine
1 cup chopped celery
14½ oz. chicken or other broth
6-oz. can bamboo shoots
14-oz. can bean sprouts
4-oz. can water chestnuts
16-oz. can baby corn
3 T. soy sauce
1½ T. cornstarch
1 T. sugar
3 T. water

Sauté onion, pepper and mushrooms in butter. When soft, add celery; sauté until nearly soft. Add meat, broth, bamboo shoots, bean sprouts, water chestnuts, baby corn and soy sauce. Simmer for 15 minutes. Blend cornstarch, sugar and water; add to vegetable mixture and cook until mixture thickens and becomes clear.

Note: You can use this recipe for any game bird, meat or fish.

Philip Stewart
Liverpool, New York

Quail with Venison Stuffing

QUAIL WITH VENISON STUFFING

10 to 12 quail, rinsed and dried
Salt
Pepper
½ cup (1 stick) butter or margarine
½ cup chopped celery
½ cup chopped onion
½ clove garlic, minced
¼ cup chopped mushrooms
2 lbs. ground venison
¼ tsp. cayenne pepper
1½ cups chicken-flavored stuffing mix or bread crumbs
¼ cup chicken broth
2 eggs, beaten
12 slices bacon

Season each quail with salt and pepper, rubbing it in; set aside. Melt butter or margarine in skillet; add celery, onion, garlic and mushrooms; sauté over medium to high heat. Add ground venison, stirring constantly. Add cayenne pepper, salt and pepper to taste, continually stirring. Moisten stuffing mix with some water and drain in separate bowl.

Add chicken broth to meat mixture and continue to stir. Add moistened stuffing and eggs to mixture; cook for 5 to 6 minutes. Stuff each quail with venison stuffing. Tie each quail's legs together or use a large toothpick. Wrap each quail in 1 slice of bacon after stuffing. Spray roasting pan with nonstick cooking spray or pour a little chicken broth on bottom of roasting pan. Add quail. Surround with any leftover stuffing. Cover and bake for 55 to 75 minutes at 350°F.

Brandon McKinniss
Harker Heights, Texas

WILD TURKEY NUGGETS

1 wild turkey breast
Garlic powder
Cajun seasoning
Black pepper
1 cup beer or milk
2 T. Worcestershire sauce
3 eggs
Flour
Pepper
Salt (optional)
Oil

Cut turkey into ½-inch boneless steaks. Sprinkle desired amount of garlic powder, Cajun seasoning and black pepper on one side of steaks. Tenderize with a meat mallet. Repeat seasoning and tenderizing for other side of steaks. Mix beer or milk, Worcestershire sauce and eggs; add meat and refrigerate overnight. Remove from marinade. Season flour with pepper and salt. Place meat in flour and cover completely. If a thicker crust is desired, dip meat back into marinade and repeat flour. Carefully cook in hot oil until done. Serve with mashed potatoes and white gravy.

Note: Venison backstraps can be used instead of turkey breast.

Karen Fussell
Austin, Texas

NUT & RAISIN STUFFING FOR GAME BIRDS

3 cups soft bread crumbs
¼ cup butter, melted
2 cups boiling water
½ cup seedless raisins
¾ cup chopped walnuts
1 egg, beaten
1 tsp. salt
⅛ tsp. pepper
½ tsp. marjoram

Sprinkle crumbs with melted butter and toss until mixed. Pour boiling water over raisins and let stand for about 5 minutes. Drain raisins and dry on paper towel. Mix raisins, nuts, egg, salt, pepper and marjoram. Toss with buttered bread crumbs.

Ray Murley
Oshawa, Ontario, Canada

PHEASANT DIVAN

2 cups cubed, cooked pheasant
2 (10-oz.) pkgs. frozen broccoli, cooked 5 minutes; drained
2 (10¾-oz.) cans cream of chicken soup
½ cup mayonnaise
½ cup sour cream
1 tsp. lemon juice
½ tsp. curry powder
½ to 1 cup grated sharp cheddar cheese
½ to 1 cup bread crumbs, browned in 2 T. butter

Arrange broccoli in shallow casserole. Place pheasant cubes over broccoli. Combine soup, mayonnaise, sour cream, lemon juice and curry powder; heat mixture and pour over meat and broccoli. Sprinkle with grated cheese and bread crumbs. Bake for 25 to 30 minutes at 350°F.

Troy Przekurat
Wheeling, Illinois

Oven-Fried Wild Turkey

Turkey, cut into pieces (removing skin is optional)
Shortening

FOR EACH POUND OF WILD TURKEY
¼ cup flour
1 tsp. paprika
¾ tsp. salt
⅛ tsp. pepper
⅛ tsp. Cajun seasoning

FOR EACH 2 POUNDS OF WILD TURKEY
1 T. melted butter
1 T. chicken broth

Heat shortening in skillet to fill ½ inch deep. Meanwhile, mix flour, paprika, salt, pepper and Cajun seasoning in a zip-top bag. Add 1 to 3 turkey pieces at a time to flour mixture and shake until coated. Place in hot shortening and brown on all sides. Place browned pieces in shallow baking pan; do not stack. Mix butter and broth; spoon over pieces. Bake at 350°F until tender and crispy. Spoon broth over turkey while baking if it appears dry. Test with fork; if fork penetrates easily, it is done. Cooking time will vary with size of pieces. Check often and spoon on broth as needed.

Duane Jones
Parkersburg, West Virginia

Louisiana Deep-Fried Wild Turkey

1 turkey breast, cut into 1-inch strips
2 cups flour
1 tsp. salt
1 tsp. pepper
½ tsp. garlic powder
½ tsp. paprika
3 T. cayenne pepper, divided
1 T. cayenne seasoning
½ cup (1 stick) butter, melted
8-oz. bottle Louisiana hot sauce
Oil for deep frying

Mix flour, salt, pepper, garlic powder, paprika, 1 tablespoon cayenne pepper and cayenne seasoning in bowl. Coat turkey strips or quail pieces in flour mixture and place in plastic bag. Save remaining flour mixture. Refrigerate meat for 1 to 2 hours.

Mix melted butter, hot sauce and remaining 2 tablespoons of the cayenne pepper in a bowl. Set aside. Heat deep fryer to hottest setting. Remove meat from refrigerator. If necessary, coat meat in reserved flour mixture, then place pieces in deep fryer for 10 to 12 minutes. Drain and place in hot sauce mixture until meat is well coated. Serve with ranch dressing for dipping sauce.

Note: This is also a great recipe for quail.

Rolland Hammond
Higginsville, Missouri

TURKEY OSCAR

2 turkey breasts
Salt
Pepper
1 cup blackened seasoning
1 cup crab claw meat or crayfish meat
1 cup brown sauce or brown gravy
6 stalks asparagus

MARTIN'S BÉARNAISE SAUCE
1 cup tarragon, chopped or dried
1 cup red wine vinegar
8 egg yolks
Salt
Pepper
2 lbs. clarified butter
Juice of 1 lemon

Season both sides of turkey breasts with salt and pepper. Coat with blackened seasoning. Put breasts on very hot, dry, ovenproof skillet. Blacken one side, flip over and top with crabmeat mixed with brown gravy. Put skillet with crabmeat into oven and bake for approximately 8 minutes at 350°F. While breasts are baking, blanch asparagus and prepare Martin's Béarnaise Sauce. To serve, arrange breast with crabmeat on plate. Arrange 6 asparagus spears around breast and top with Béarnaise sauce.

Mix tarragon and vinegar in stainless pot; bring to a boil. Reduce until tarragon is barely moist. Be careful! Put yolks in stainless bowl; add 3 tablespoons of tarragon reduction. Add 2 pinches of salt and pepper; whisk until smooth. Place bowl over pot of boiling water, whisking constantly until eggs start to get hot and thicken slightly. Remove from heat and slowly add clarified butter, whisking until smooth and creamy. Add juice of lemon and more salt and pepper, if desired. If sauce breaks or separates, add 3 teaspoons hot water and slowly add sauce to it, whisking slowly to mix. It will become smooth.

Mark Martin
Covington, Ohio

Turkey Oscar

PINEAPPLE-SAGE GAME HENS

4 game hens, cleaned and giblets removed
Salt
Pepper
4 cups rice pilaf or bread stuffing
20-oz. can pineapple chunks with juice
Zest of 1 orange
1 cup chardonnay
½ cup brandy
½ cup finely chopped fresh sage
2 T. parsley
2 T. basil

Rub birds inside and out with salt and pepper. Stuff with rice pilaf or bread stuffing; set aside. In saucepan, combine pineapple chunks and juice, zest, wine, brandy, sage, parsley and basil. Bring to a boil, stirring. Reduce by one-third. Liberally cover birds with pineapple sauce, reserving half of the sauce. Bake for 1 to 1¼ hours at 350°F. Remove birds and glaze with remaining sauce.

Tip: Cover wing tips and leg ends with foil to prevent burning.

Mark Martin
Covington, Ohio

TWO-SMILES RANCH STIR-FRY QUAIL WRAPS

6 quail or upland game birds
15-oz. can chicken broth or 1 bouillon
    cube
4 T. freshly grated gingerroot
2 large white onions, finely chopped
8 cloves garlic, finely chopped or minced
7 T. extra virgin olive oil
2 oz. white wine
1 serrano or jalapeño pepper, chopped
2 carrots, chopped
3 T. cilantro, chopped
5 oz. water chestnuts, drained
6 T. light soy sauce
1 tsp. coarsely ground black pepper
2 tsp. cayenne pepper
3 pinches of salt
Head of iceberg or romaine lettuce

Bring broth to a boil in large pot and add quail. Boil for 5 minutes or until partially done. Remove quail from broth. Let cool, then pull skin off meat and meat from bones. Discard carcass; reserve broth.

Mince quail into small pea-size pieces and add gingerroot. Marinate for 15 minutes. Keep mixture cool. Place onion and garlic in large skillet. Add olive oil and increase heat to medium. Cook until onions are slightly clear. Turn heat to low and add reserved broth and white wine. Reduce to about half the volume. Add pepper, carrots, cilantro, water chestnuts, soy sauce, black pepper, cayenne pepper and salt. Simmer for 10 minutes. Increase heat to medium and let quail and gingerroot cook for 10 minutes or until liquid reduces to a heavy sauce.

To serve: Remove core from lettuce and open each leaf to be an individual wrap. Soak wraps in ice water to crisp. Place a spoonful of quail mixture on each lettuce wrap.

Terry McCullough
Dallas, Texas

GROUSE & VEGETABLE STROGANOFF

1 cooked grouse, cut up
1½ cups frozen broccoli, cauliflower and carrots
1½ cups sliced fresh mushrooms
2 cups chicken broth or 2 cups broth from grouse if boiled
1 T. chopped fresh marjoram leaves or 1 tsp. dried marjoram
¼ tsp. pepper
1 large onion, sliced
3 to 3½ cups uncooked egg noodles
8 oz. sour cream
⅓ cup water
2 T. flour

Heat frozen vegetables, mushrooms, broth, marjoram, pepper, onion and noodles over high heat in medium skillet to boiling; reduce heat. Cover and simmer about 8 to 10 minutes or until noodles and vegetables are tender, stirring frequently. Stir in grouse. Mix sour cream, water and flour; stir into grouse mixture. Heat to boiling. Let boil for 1 to 2 minutes, stirring constantly.

Robert C. Shenk
Paterson, New Jersey

WILD GAME OMELET

½ cup leftover game or bird meat
6 eggs
½ cup butter
Salt
Pepper
½ cup chopped green onion
Grated cheese (optional)

Mix eggs, butter, salt and pepper; fry as for an ordinary omelet. In saucepan, combine meat and onion; heat thoroughly. When omelet is done, spoon game mixture over top; fold and serve hot. Add grated cheese, if desired.

Michael and Kimberly Zion
Julesburg, Colorado

PHEASANT POT PIE

3 to 4 cups diced, cooked pheasant, quail, dove, grouse or rabbit, reserve pan drippings
2 to 3 cups peas/carrots mixture
6 small to medium potatoes, cooked and cubed
15-oz. can whole kernel corn, drained
15-oz. can chicken broth
1-oz. pkg. chicken gravy mix
1 T. cornstarch
Salt (optional)
2 to 3 deep-dish 8- or 9-inch pie shells
2 to 3 cups prepared mashed potatoes
1 cup shredded cheddar cheese

In large bowl, mix pheasant, peas/carrots, potatoes and corn. Blend pan drippings, broth and gravy mix in separate pan; simmer slowly, stirring frequently. Add cornstarch to thicken. Salt to taste. Fill pie shells ⅔ full with meat and vegetable mixture. Pour thickened gravy over meat mixture and cover. Bake for 45 minutes at 350°F. Top with mashed potatoes; sprinkle with shredded cheese and bake for an additional 15 minutes or until pie crust is light brown and cheese is melted. Let stand for 15 minutes before serving.

Tom Held
Butte, Montana

Chapter 6

WATERFOWL

Here is a meat all its own—sometimes mild, sometimes as wild as the wetlands and waterways that ducks and geese call home. There are secrets to making great meals from waterfowl, and you'll find those secrets right here—recipes from masters of the trade, fellow members who know how to shoot a duck or goose and then enjoy it on the table.

TERIYAKI GOOSE STIR-FRY

2 Canada goose breast fillets (from 1 goose)
4 T. baking soda
½ cup teriyaki sauce
¼ cup light soy sauce
1 clove garlic, crushed
8 T. cooking oil, divided
2 medium onions, chopped (approx. 2 cups)
1 clove garlic, minced or thinly chopped
3 large carrots, sliced thin (approx. 2 cups)
Large broccoli crown, cut into bite-size chunks (approx. 2 cups)
½ head cauliflower, cut into bite-size chunks (approx. 2½ cups)
½ red pepper, chopped or cut into thin strips (approx. ⅔ cup)

Slice each breast lengthwise into three strips. In casserole, stir baking soda into 3 tablespoons cold water until dissolved. Add strips of meat and marinate for 24 hours or overnight in refrigerator. This will reduce gamey taste. Discard water and rinse goose in cold water. Trim fat, gristle and bloodshot meat from strips. Make sure to check for and remove any shot. Don't skimp on cleaning up the meat; there is a lot of meat here.

Mix teriyaki sauce, soy sauce and crushed garlic. Add to meat; stir well and let soak while you prepare vegetables.

Put 5 tablespoons cooking oil into a deep skillet and heat to 350°F. When oil is hot, add onions and minced garlic. Cook until onions turn golden brown. Add meat with sauce. Cook until meat is thoroughly browned, stirring frequently. Remove meat and sauce and place in a covered casserole.

Add remaining 3 tablespoons cooking oil to skillet. Add carrots and stir-fry for approximately 2 minutes. Add broccoli and cauliflower; stir-fry for another 2 minutes. Add red pepper and stir-fry for an additional minute. Add meat and sauce to vegetable mixture and stir-fry for 2 minutes. Serve over rice or your favorite pasta.

Note: Times are approximate depending on how crispy or soft you prefer your vegetables. Cooking in the order listed gives you a uniform degree of doneness since carrots take the most time and red pepper the least. There is no limit to the vegetables you can use. Zucchini, sliced white or red cabbage are great alternatives. I add whatever I have on hand from the garden or refrigerator.

Bernie Kaplun
Okanagan Falls, British Columbia, Canada

DUCK BREASTS WITH ORANGE MARMALADE

Breasts of 3 ducks, boned and filleted
⅓ cup water
16-oz. jar orange marmalade

Place duck breasts in Crock-Pot. Mix water and marmalade; pour over meat. Cover and cook on low for at least 6 hours. Meat will be tender and moist. Lay meat on plate. If desired, pour sauce over meat before serving.

Dave Isenberger
Omaha, Nebraska

Two Ducks & a Goose

2 ducks, plucked and cleaned
1 goose, plucked and cleaned
2 (6-oz.) boxes Original Uncle Ben's
   Wild Rice
2 to 4 slices bacon
Salt
Pepper
½ (12-oz.) can beer
½ (14½-oz.) can beef broth

Place rice in roaster pan. Stuff birds with some of the rice or other stuffing, if desired. Place birds on bed of rice. Lay bacon over each bird. Season with salt and pepper as you would a steak. Add beer and broth to rice bed. Cover and bake for 30 to 35 minutes at 350°F. Uncover and cook at 450°F or broil for 5 to 10 minutes until skin is browned. Rice should be moist but not soupy. Slice birds and serve rice from roaster.

Note: Duck will be medium rare. Cook longer, if desired. Beer accents flavor of rice. Change brands as desired for flavor.

Daniel Tatem
Dover, New Hampshire

Duck Nuggets

4 duck breasts or 2 goose breasts
1 cup soy sauce
1 cup dry white wine
1 cup water
2 tsp. ginger
4 cloves garlic, minced or ½ tsp. garlic
   powder

Combine soy sauce, wine, water, ginger and garlic. Add duck or goose breasts and marinate in glass bowl for 24 hours. Remove meat from marinade and grill for 10 to 15 minutes on each side or until done. Cut into 1-inch squares. Can be served as a main dish or as a snack after cooling. Also great as an appetizer.

Chris Sandmark
Casper, Wyoming

Golden Goose

Goose breast, filleted
1 to 2 eggs, beaten
Salt
Pepper
Finely crushed saltine crackers
Oil

Slice chunks of breast against the grain. Pound meat to about ⅜-inch thick and 5-inches in diameter. Dip in eggs, season with salt and pepper, dredge in cracker crumbs. Fry in small amount of oil until golden brown. Makes a mean sandwich or a main meat dish. Tastes like tenderloin.

Randy Hoey
Marshall, Missouri

BLACKBERRY DUCK

2 large ducks (½ breast per person)
¼ cup finely chopped white onion
1 cup sliced mushrooms
½ cup (1 stick) butter
Seasoned salt
Flour
1 to 2 cups blackberry wine

Remove meat from each side of breast and cut into ½-inch strips. Sauté onions and mushrooms in butter until onions are tender. Sprinkle meat strips with seasoned salt, coat with flour. Add to onion mixture and brown on all sides; set aside. Reposition browned meat strips back in pan in lattice pattern. Add wine mixed with water to cover meat. Simmer for 1 hour on low heat. Place meat strips on plate and spoon gravy over pieces.

Note: This cooks best in cast-iron skillet.

Gary W. Hart
Edmond, Oklahoma

DUCKS & GEESE

Ducks or geese
Dressing
Butter or margarine
Salt
Pepper
Water

Clean and rinse. Pat dry inside and out. Use your favorite dressing recipe. Stuff bird. Tie legs and tail together. Rub each bird with butter or margarine; season with salt and pepper. Place in roasting pan, add water and cover with aluminum foil. Bake for 1 hour at 350°F or until done.

William Robinson
Newark, Delaware

CAJUN DUCK & ANDOUILLE SAUSAGE GUMBO

3 large ducks (4 or 5 teal or small ducks)
1 lb. Andouille sausage or other sausage of choice
3 T. vegetable oil
3 large onions
⅓ cup chopped shallots
⅓ cup chopped green bell pepper
¼ cup chopped celery
2 cloves garlic, minced
1 T. cayenne pepper
2 T. seasoned salt
3 to 4 T. Worcestershire sauce
3 T. ground sassafras leaves
1 T. brown gravy sauce

Debone breast of ducks, quarter legs and wings, save gizzards and livers, if desired. Cut sausage into ½-inch rounds. Heat oil in large heavy pot or Dutch oven on high heat. Add onions; brown while stirring. Add shallots, green bell pepper, celery and garlic and brown for 5 to 7 minutes. Add duck pieces and sausage to mixture and stir vigorously for 2 to 4 minutes. Add 6 to 8 cups of water and bring to a boil. Add cayenne pepper, seasoned salt, Worcestershire sauce, sassafras leaves and brown gravy sauce. Boil for 2 to 3 minutes; reduce heat and simmer for 1½ hours or until desired tenderness. Serve over white or wild rice. A cold potato salad and hot French bread make great accompaniments.

Note: The first time you prepare this, season to your taste as it might be a bit strong for those not accustomed to Cajun dishes.

Jason Matherne
Houma, Louisiana

EASIEST DUCK BREASTS

Boneless duck breast fillets from several ducks, sliced into strips
Italian salad dressing
Bacon

Marinate breast meat in dressing for a couple of hours. Remove from liquid. Place a piece of bacon on each breast strip, roll up and secure with toothpick. Place on hot grill or in hot pan and cook until bacon is just cooked. Serve immediately. Good cold too.

Dan Molaski
Montrose, Michigan

BARBECUED GOOSE IN A CROCK-POT

2 or 3 boneless goose breast fillets
16-oz. bottle ketchup
12-oz. can cola
1.4-oz. envelope dry onion soup mix

Put meat in Crock-Pot. Mix ketchup, cola and soup mix. Pour over meat. Slow cook on low for 6 to 8 hours. Mixture becomes a barbecue sauce and meat will be tender.

Note: Substitute duck or any other meat of choice for the goose.

Jon Kalka
Pembina, North Dakota

COARSE PEPPER GOOSE STEAK

Goose breast, bones removed
Garlic powder
Coarsely ground black pepper
Minced onion
Mushrooms, sliced
Butter
Gravy mix, prepared as directed

Place goose breast between pieces of plastic wrap. Pound both sides until thin. Sprinkle with garlic powder, any other spices you want and lots of coarse pepper; press spices into meat. Fry for 2 minutes on each side; set aside.

Sauté onion and mushrooms in butter. Place goose breasts, onion and mushrooms in baking dish. Prepare gravy; add enough gravy to cover meat. Cover dish and bake for 20 minutes at 350°F.

James Marchini
Copper Center, Arkansas

Duck or Goose Kabobs

DUCK OR GOOSE KABOBS

Duck or goose breast, boned and cut into
    bite-size pieces
Bacon or sausage
Mushrooms
Pineapple chunks
Salt
Lemon pepper

Place a piece of duck or goose on a skewer, then a piece of bacon or sausage, followed by a mushroom and a pineapple chunk. Repeat. Lightly season with salt and lemon pepper. Lay kabob over briquette bucket or grill, turning frequently, for about 15 minutes. Do not overcook. Meat should be light and pink.

We make these right in the duck blind since we need briquettes for heat anyway. A skillet will fit on top of a 5-gallon bucket.

John Johnston
Moose Lake, Washington

SMOKE-ROASTED CHERRY/LIME DUCK

1 whole duck or 4 duck breasts, cleaned,
    skinned and all shot removed
1½ cups cherry wine
¼ cup Worcestershire sauce
4 to 8 whole limes
1 to 2 (1-lb.) pkgs. bacon
18-oz. bottle barbecue sauce

In glass bowl, combine wine and Worcestershire sauce. Cut limes in half and squeeze juice into bowl; stir. Rinse duck and check again for shot. Place breasts or whole duck breast-side down in wine mixture. Cover and refrigerate for 8 to 12 hours or more depending on personal taste. This mixture will give the duck an exquisite taste. Remove duck from marinade and wrap it completely with strips of bacon, securing with toothpicks. Place duck on generous-size piece of aluminum foil. Lightly and evenly cover entire duck with barbecue sauce. Wrap foil over duck securely.

If using smoker, leave a small top of foil open and cook over medium to high heat for several hours. If using grill, place foil-wrapped duck on top rack over medium-high heat for at least 2 hours, rotating duck every 15 to 20 minutes. For last hour or so, add some flavored smoke pellets to grill and open top of foil over duck. Serve with buttered, sliced, new potatoes, green beans and cooked baby carrots.

Brad Ouart
Tulsa, Oklahoma

GOLDEN GOOSE

Boneless, skinless breast halves of 1 goose
1 lb. bacon, sliced thick
Pepper
2 (10¾-oz.) cans golden mushroom soup
Water

Cut goose breasts into 1 x 2-inch pieces. Cut bacon into strips and wrap around pieces of goose, using toothpicks to hold bacon in place. Sprinkle with pepper. Fry on medium heat for 30 minutes. Add soup and water. Cover and cook on low for 2 to 3 hours.

Irving Santti
Baraga, Michigan

CROCK-POT GOOSE

1 goose breast, sliced thin
2 cups water
2 medium potatoes, peeled and diced
2 medium carrots, peeled and diced
½ cup medium barley
14-oz. can chicken broth
1 medium onion, chopped
4-oz. can mushrooms
14-oz. can French-cut green beans
½ cup almond slivers

Combine goose breast, water, potatoes, carrots, barley, broth, onion, mushrooms, green beans and almonds in Crock-Pot and cook for 8 to 10 hours on low heat.

W. Michael and Denise Toon
Trout Run, Pennsylvania

GARLIC ROASTED DUCK

3 large whole ducks, skins on
½ cup chicken broth
¼ cup olive oil
½ tsp. paprika
Salt
Pepper
15 to 20 cloves garlic, peeled and left whole

In large casserole, place ducks side by side, breast-side up. Pour chicken broth and olive oil over ducks. Sprinkle with paprika, salt and pepper. Place garlic on and around ducks. Cover dish with aluminum foil and place lid on top. Cook for 6 hours at 200°F. Meat will fall off bones. Serve with wild rice, asparagus tips and French bread. Gravy can be made from pan drippings and poured over top of ducks when served.

Geoff Maynard
Arlington, Tennessee

WILD GOOSE ROAST

10- to 12-lb. wild goose, cleaned and
dressed
1 large apple, chopped
1 large onion, chopped
1 cup chopped celery

STUFFING
7 cups dry bread crumbs
3 cups chopped apples
1 cup scalded raisins
1 T. sage
½ tsp. salt

SEASONINGS
1 T. flour
1 tsp. salt
1 T. sage
1 tsp. paprika
1 tsp. pepper

BASTING MIXTURE
1 cup clear apple juice
1 cup grapefruit juice
½ cup prune juice

Wash goose thoroughly and pat dry. Mix chopped apple, onion and celery and place in cavity. Let stand overnight in covered roaster in a cool place or refrigerator. Remove apple mixture next day and discard.

Mix bread crumbs, chopped apples, raisins, sage and salt. Fill cavity with stuffing. Close cavity.

Mix flour, salt, sage, paprika and pepper. Rub well into outer skin of goose. If any mixture is left, sprinkle over breast. Place goose in uncovered roaster and bake for 15 minutes at 400°F. Reduce heat to 325°F and cook until tender, allowing 20 minutes per pound after the first half hour.

Mix apple, grapefruit and prune juices. Baste goose every 5 minutes during cooking.

Ray Murley
Oshawa, Ontario, Canada

PLUM DUCK

4 duck breasts
Onion, sliced
Apple, sliced
Plums, strained
1 medium onion, chopped
¼ cup butter
6-oz. can frozen lemonade
⅓ cup chili sauce
¼ cup soy sauce
1 tsp. Worcestershire sauce
1 tsp. ginger
2 tsp. prepared mustard
Bacon slices

Stuff ducks with sliced onion and apple in cavity. Wrap in foil and bake at 350°F until done. While ducks are baking, put plums through strainer. Sauté chopped onions in butter. Add lemonade and plum purée; stir. Add chili sauce, soy sauce, Worcestershire sauce, ginger and mustard; stir. Simmer for 30 minutes. Remove ducks from oven and unwrap. Slice meat off bones and place in shallow pan with apple and onion from cavity. Pour sauce over duck. Place bacon slices on top of duck pieces. Turn oven off and place pan in oven for 15 minutes.

Dave Henry Nyquist
Dent, Minnesota

Deep-Fried Goose

2 goose breasts, sliced ⅜-inch thick
3 T. sugar
½ tsp. salt
1 egg
1 T. baking powder
2 cups milk, divided
Cornflake crumbs

Mix sugar, salt, egg and baking powder with 1 cup milk; stir until smooth. Add remaining 1 cup milk and mix well. Dip meat into mixture, then roll in crumbs. Cook in deep fryer until done and serve immediately.

Mixture can also be used for deer steak that has been put through a tenderizer.

Don Rethman
Jackson Center, Ohio

Deep-Fried Goose

Duck Breast with Wild Blueberry Sauce

4 to 6 duck breasts, boned and skin removed
   (1 breast per person)
½ cup red wine
1 tsp. garlic
Salt
Pepper
1 T. olive oil (enough to coat bottom of pan)
3 T. wild blueberry preserves
2 T. butter
⅓ cup heavy cream (optional)

Rinse duck breasts and pat dry with paper towel. Mix red wine and garlic together in glass dish or bowl; add duck breasts. Season with salt and pepper. Marinate 2 to 3 hours or overnight. Turn occasionally to ensure that they are evenly marinated.

Heat olive oil in heavy skillet. Add duck breasts one at a time and sauté for 3 to 5 minutes or until just done (medium-rare to medium). Duck breasts should be nicely browned like a filet mignon or sirloin when done; remove from heat and keep warm on platter. Add blueberry preserves to pan and reduce heat to simmer. When hot and bubbly, add butter and simmer until smooth and syrupy. Add cream, if desired. Slice duck breasts across grain and arrange on plate. Pour a little blueberry sauce over top. Serve with wild rice or rice pilaf and a delicate vegetable such as white or baby asparagus.

Jon Gross
Clay Springs, Arizona

Goose Fit for a King

4 boneless goose breast halves, cut into finger
   steak-size pieces
1 cup whipping cream
10¾-oz. can cream of mushroom soup
4-oz. can mushroom pieces
Garlic salt
Pepper

Combine whipping cream, soup, mushrooms, garlic salt and pepper; mix thoroughly. Place goose pieces in greased baking pan. Pour soup mixture over top. Bake, uncovered, for 1½ hours at 350°F. Liquid can be used to make gravy for over rice or potatoes.

Jeff McCoy
Forsyth, Montana

BAKED DUCK WITH BARBECUE SAUCE

2 ducks, skinned and disjointed
1 cup wine vinegar
Salt
Pepper
½ cup flour
½ cup fat

BARBECUE SAUCE
1 large onion, minced
1 clove garlic, minced
4 celery ribs, finely chopped
4 T. salad oil
2 cups consommé
1 bay leaf
1 cup tomato juice
2 tsp. Worcestershire sauce
4 peppercorns
1 sprig parsley, minced

Cut duck into serving-size pieces. Place duck pieces in glass dish. Add wine vinegar and enough water to cover. Marinate in refrigerator for several hours or overnight. Drain duck pieces and dry them. Season each piece with salt and pepper; roll in flour. Brown pieces in hot fat in skillet; transfer to baking dish.

Cook onion, garlic and celery in oil until tender but not brown. Add consommé, bay leaf, tomato juice, Worcestershire sauce, peppercorns and parsley. Simmer for 30 minutes. Pour over duck pieces in baking dish. Bake for 3 hours at 350°F or until meat is tender.

William Ostermeyer
Kilbourne, Illinois

DUCK À L'ORANGE

2 duck breasts, skins on
Salt
Pepper
Juice of 2 oranges
½ cup chardonnay
¼ tsp. thyme
¼ tsp. parsley
¼ tsp. basil
¼ cup brandy
Zest of 1 orange

Season breasts with salt and pepper. In sizzling hot ovenproof skillet, lay breasts skin-side down. Sear until brown. Flip meat over and bake at 400°F for 5 to 8 minutes or until medium-rare or rare. In separate pan, combine orange juice, chardonnay, thyme, parsley, basil and brandy. Boil and reduce by one-half. Remove breasts from pan and let rest for 5 minutes. Slice on the bias and serve over mesclun mix (salad mix). Top with sauce, sprinkle with orange zest and garnish with chive flowers and basil leaves.

Mark Martin
Covington, Ohio

Chapter 7

JERKY, SAUSAGE & SMOKED MEATS

Who says you have to cook everything at the stove or grill and then sit down and eat it for dinner? The ideas here avoid that notion, presenting methods and recipes for creating jerky and sausage from (as well as smoking) the game you bring home. Give some of these ideas a try, and add some variety to the way you complete each hunt!

Meat Jerky*   *Information submitted by Russell Tait of Laramie, Wyoming*

Jerky is made by drying thin strips of lean meat to about one-fourth its original weight. Although drying in the oven or dehydrator decreases the risk of producing contaminated jerky, illnesses in recent years due to Salmonella and *Escherichia coli* in homemade jerky products have raised questions about the safety of all methods of drying jerky products at home.

One method for ensuring the adequate destruction of *E. coli* during jerky preparation is to pre-cook the meat to 160°F before drying. This method is currently recommended by the Meat and Poultry Hotline (1-800-535-4555) of the U.S. Department of Agriculture (USDA). But pre-cooking creates a product that is different from traditional jerky and therefore may not be well received by consumers. Also, the product may not dry evenly throughout because of case-hardening on the outside surface.

As alternatives, the jerky preparation methods given below were developed as part of a joint project between the Department of Food Science and Human Nutrition and the Department of Animal Science at Colorado State University, and were found effective in reducing numbers of *E. coli* in inoculated samples.

Jerky Preparation

Use only lean meats in excellent condition. Round, flank and chuck steak, rump roast, brisket and cross rib are good choices. Highly marbled and fatty cuts do not work as well. When preparing jerky products, keep raw meats and their juices away from other foods. Remove any thick connective tissue and gristle from fresh meat. Trim off visible fat with a sharp knife. Fat becomes rancid quickly and causes the development of off-flavors during drying or storage. Freeze meat in moisture-proof paper or plastic wrap until firm but not solid.

Slice the slightly-frozen meat (on a clean cutting board) into long thin strips, approximately ⅛ to ¼ inch thick, 1 to 1½ inches wide and 4 to 10 inches long. Slice with the grain if a chewy jerky is preferred; slice across the grain for a more tender, brittle jerky. Lay the strips out in a single layer on a clean and sanitized smooth surface (cutting board, countertop, baking sheet). Flatten the strips with a rolling pin so they are fairly uniform in thickness.

Note: *Always wash and sanitize cutting boards, utensils and counters with hot, soapy water before and after any contact with raw meat or juices. To make a sanitizing solution, use 1 teaspoon of household chlorine bleach per quart of water.*

Test for Dryness

Properly dried jerky is chewy and leathery. It will be as brittle as a green stick, but won't snap like a dry stick. To test for dryness, remove a strip of jerky from the oven or dehydrator. Let cool slightly, then bend the jerky; it should crack, but not break, when bent.

When jerky is sufficiently dry, remove the strips from the drying racks to a clean surface. Pat off any beads of oil with absorbent paper toweling and let cool.

Jerky Storage

Place cooled jerky strips in an airtight plastic food bag or jar with a tight-fitting lid. Pack jerky with the least possible amount of air trapped in the container. Too much air causes off-flavors and allows rancidity to develop. Label and date packages. Store containers of jerky in a cool, dry, dark place or in the refrigerator or freezer.

Properly dried jerky will keep for approximately 1 month in a sealed container at room temperature. It will keep for 3 to 6 months in the refrigerator and up to 1 year in the freezer. Check occasionally to be sure no mold is forming.

* This information developed by Pat Kendall, PhD, RD, Extension Specialist and Professor, Department of Food Science and Human Nutrition, and John Sofos, PhD, Professor, Department of Animal Sciences, Colorado State University, July 2000.

Hot Pickle Cure Preparation Method for Jerky

Ingredients per 2 pounds of lean meat slices:

Pickling Spices
1½ T. salt
1 T. sugar
1 tsp. black pepper

Hot Pickle Brine
¾ cup salt
½ cup sugar
2 T. black pepper

Place lean meat slices (see Jerky Preparation, opposite page) on clean baking sheets or flat pans. Evenly distribute half of the pickling spices on the top surfaces of the meat slices. Press spices into meat with rubber mallet or meat tenderizer. Turn slices and repeat on opposite sides. Cover and refrigerate for 24 hours.

In large kettle, combine hot pickle brine with 1 gallon water. Stir to dissolve salt and sugar and bring to a slow boil (175°F). Place a few meat slices at a time in a steamer basket and lower into brine. Simmer for 1½ to 2 minutes, stirring occasionally to make sure all pieces are immersed.

Preheat dehydrator or oven to 145°F or 150°F. Lift basket out of kettle and drain liquid. Using clean tongs, remove meat pieces and place flat, without touching each other, on clean dehydrator trays, oven racks or other drying trays. Place in preheated dehydrator, leaving enough open space on racks for air to circulate around the strips. Repeat the process until all meat pieces have been pickled in the brine solution and placed in the dehydrator. Let strips dry for 8 to 12 hours, or until the slices are adequately dry (see test for dryness, opposite page).

Russell Tait
Laramie, Wyoming

Acidified Marinade Preparation Method for Jerky

Ingredients per 2 pounds of lean meat slices:
½ cup soy sauce
1 T. Worcestershire sauce
¼ tsp. black pepper
¼ tsp. garlic powder
½ tsp. onion powder
1 tsp. hickory smoked salt
3 tsp. ascorbic acid or 1 tsp. citric acid crystals

Combine all marinade ingredients and place in a 1-gallon zip-top bag. Add lean meat slices (see Jerky Preparation) to bag; seal bag and massage pieces to thoroughly distribute marinade over all meat strips. Refrigerate bag for 1 hour only. Marinating for a longer period is not recommended as it may provide time for E. coli bacteria to become acid-resistant, if present.

Remove meat slices from bag and place flat, without touching each other, on clean dehydrator trays, oven racks or other drying trays. Dry at 145°F to 150°F for 8 to 12 hours, or until pieces are adequately dry (Test for dryness, opposite page).

Russel Tait
Laramie, Wyoming

Venison Jerky with Barbecue Sauce

2 lbs. venison steak, fat removed and sliced into
  ¼-inch strips
⅓ cup soy sauce
⅓ cup Worcestershire sauce
2 tsp. liquid smoke
1 tsp. onion powder
½ tsp. garlic
1 tsp. salt
1 tsp. pepper
3 tsp. hot sauce (cayenne pepper sauce)
4 tsp. barbecue sauce

Place meat in jar or bowl with lid. Mix soy sauce, Worcestershire sauce, liquid smoke, onion powder, garlic, salt, pepper, hot sauce and barbecue sauce; pour over steak strips. Mix, cover and marinate in refrigerator for 24 hours. Drain meat and pat dry with paper towels. Place meat on dehydrator trays or insert toothpicks into ends of meat strips and hang from oven rack. Dry for 4 to 6 hours at 140°F to 160°F.

Bill Thrune
Dakota, Minnesota

Spicy Wild Turkey Sausage

2½ lbs. wild turkey meat, diced
½ cup chopped garlic
6 tsp. chili powder
4 T. paprika
2 tsp. cayenne pepper
2 tsp. ground cumin
2 tsp. salt
1 tsp. crushed red pepper
1 tsp. dried oregano
1 tsp. dried thyme
1 tsp. freshly ground black pepper
2 tsp. onion powder
½ tsp. garlic powder

Prepare smoker. Place turkey in large mixing bowl. In small mixing bowl, combine garlic, chili powder, paprika, cayenne pepper, cumin, salt, red pepper, oregano, thyme, black pepper, onion powder and garlic powder. Mix well and pour over turkey. Toss turkey with seasoning blend until mixed well. Cover and refrigerate for 24 hours. Grind meat twice in meat grinder fitted with a ½-inch die. A food processor could be used to grind the meat. Stuff half the mixture into 1 ½-inch casings, forming 6-inch links. Form the remaining into 3 (½-pound) patties. Sausage can be used either fresh or smoked. For smoked sausage, place sausage in smoker and cook for 10 to 15 minutes. Makes about 2¾ pounds.

George Transue Jr.
Bates City, Missouri

Goose Breakfast Sausage

For each pound of meat:
1½ tsp. salt
⅛ tsp. white pepper
⅛ tsp. black pepper
1½ tsp. nutmeg
⅛ tsp. ginger
1½ tsp. thyme
1½ tsp. cayenne pepper (optional)
1½ oz. ice water

Mix salt, white pepper, black pepper, nutmeg, ginger, thyme, cayenne pepper and water with ground meat. Stuff sausage in 22-mm casings or make patties. Freezes well for up to 3 months.

Tip: Use only clean meat that is free of blood. It is fatty enough that you won't have to add domestic pork. Chill meat thoroughly to about 35°F. Grind using a ³⁄₁₆-inch plate.

Roger Penrod
Muskego, Wisconsin

MACHACADO CON HUEVOS
(DRIED SHREDDED MEAT WITH BREAKFAST EGGS)

MACHACADO
½ cup shredded meat
1 to 2 T. vegetable oil
¼ cup chopped or thinly sliced onion
1 to 2 serrano peppers, cut into small thin slices
½ cup chopped fresh or canned tomato
4 eggs, lightly beaten

*Simple dried jerky (carne seca) is made by adding salt and pepper to the meat slices. When the meat is dried, pound it with a hammer or meat tenderizer until you can shred it with your hands. **Note:** I have never made this from ground meat; I'm not sure it would work.*

Fry shredded meat in oil. Add onion and cook lightly. Add peppers and tomatoes to pan and cook briefly. Add eggs and stir until eggs are set. Serve with hot flour tortillas. Top with picante sauce if desired.

Robert Solis
Edinburg, Texas

UNCLE DAN'S SWEET VENISON BOLOGNA

10 lbs. venison
½ cup Morton Tender Quick
⅔ cup packed brown sugar
1 cup non-fat dry milk
2 T. fine white pepper
4 tsp. whole mustard seed
2 tsp. crushed red peppers
2 tsp. Prague Powder #1 cure
1 qt. ice water mixed with 2 tsp. liquid smoke
2¼-inch fibrous casings

Grind meat once. Combine Tender Quick, brown sugar, dry milk, white pepper, mustard seeds, red peppers and Prague Powder. Mix well with meat. Add ice water mixture and mix well. Grind meat second time. Stuff into casings. Refrigerate overnight. Place sticks on racks and baking sheets. Bake for 3 to 4 hours at 200°F until meat is 160°F. Chill immediately in ice water to 100°F to prevent shrinking. Dry and refrigerate.

Daniel L. Stover
Spring Mills, Pennsylvania

VENISON BRATWURST IN CURRANT JELLY & MUSTARD GLAZE

1 lb. venison brats
2 (12-oz.) jars currant jelly
8-oz. bottle mustard

Pre-cook venison brats and slice into ¼- to ½-inch pieces. Mix currant jelly and mustard. Put brats in frying pan, add jelly-mustard mixture. Cook uncovered on very low heat for 5 to 6 hours or until glaze has thickened. Serve warm.

Bob Pozner
Minnetonka, Minnesota

Mike's Spicy Jerky

2 lbs. meat (deer, bear, elk, caribou), cut into 6 x 1 x 1-inch strips (easy to cut if still partially frozen)
1 cup soy sauce
1 T. liquid smoke
1 T. cider vinegar
3 T. Worcestershire sauce
1 T. White Wine Worcestershire sauce (optional)
2 T. cayenne hot sauce
1 T. Tabasco sauce
2 T. coarse steak seasoning
1 T. balsamic vinegar (optional)
½ tsp. black pepper
1 tsp. garlic salt

In medium bowl, mix soy sauce, liquid smoke, cider vinegar, Worcestershire sauces, hot sauce, Tabasco sauce, steak seasoning, balsamic vinegar, pepper and garlic salt.

Stagger meat strips in 8 x 8-inch plastic container; cover with marinade. Cover and refrigerate for at least 24 hours; turning container as many times as possible.

Place meat strips in dehydrator for 24 hours, in water smoker for 1 to 2 hours or in 125°F to 150°F oven for 6 to 8 hours. Drying times may vary. (Dehydrator works best.)

For the hot pepper lover, sprinkle meat with cayenne or habanero powder before drying.

Michael Shultz
West Chester, Pennsylvania

Poor Man's Sausage

4 lbs. ground venison
1 lb. hamburger
3 tsp. pepper
2 tsp. whole mustard seed
2½ tsp. smoked hickory salt
1½ tsp. garlic salt
5 tsp. Morton Tender Quick (no substitute)

Combine venison, hamburger, pepper, mustard seed, hickory salt, garlic salt and Tender Quick. Mix well in glass bowl; cover and refrigerate for 24 hours. Mix again. Roll into 5 loaves. Bake in broiler pan for 8 hours at 150°F. Refrigerate for 2 days before cutting.

Edward Sibole
Gerrardstown, West Virginia

Moose Meat Jerky

1½ to 2 lbs. boneless moose steak, partially frozen
¼ cup soy sauce
1 T. Worcestershire sauce
¼ tsp. pepper
¼ tsp. garlic powder
½ tsp. hickory smoke salt

Cut meat into 1-inch-wide strips ¼ to ½ inch thick while still partially frozen. Mix all ingredients together in a stainless steel mixing bowl; cover tightly and refrigerate for at least 5 hours, stirring and/or shaking occasionally. Preheat oven to lowest temperature. Arrange meat close together on oven rack and bake for 4 to 6 hours, checking often. Alternative: use smoker in lieu of oven.

Roger Laye
Prince George, British Columbia, Canada

Mike's Spicy Jerky

PEPPERONI

4 lbs. ground venison (ground twice)
1 lb. ground hot sausage
3 tsp. lemon pepper
1 tsp. black pepper
2½ tsp. liquid smoke
2 tsp. garlic flakes
5 tsp. salt
½ tsp. red pepper flakes
2½ tsp. whole mustard seed

Mix venison, hot sausage, lemon pepper, black pepper, liquid smoke, garlic flakes, salt, red pepper flakes and mustard seed. Refrigerate for 24 hours. Roll out in lengths like pepperoni. Cook for 7 hours at 200°F on broiler pan. Package and freeze.

Virginia Stape
Stanley, New York

WILL'S HOMEMADE LIVER SAUSAGE

2 to 3 lbs. venison, elk or pork liver, skinned and cut into chunks
4 to 5 lbs. pork shoulder, untrimmed or pork that is fatty
1 onion, cut in half
1 hamburger bun
1 tsp. sage
2 T. sugar
1 tsp. allspice
1 tsp. marjoram
1 T. salt
½ tsp. pepper
¼ tsp. cinnamon

In separate pans, cover meat with water and cook until done. Save juice from pork shoulder. Skim off scum when cooking liver.

Grind meat and onion; add bun. Mix sage, sugar, allspice, marjoram, salt, pepper and cinnamon together; blend into ground meat. Add juice from pork shoulder to make sausage moist. Package in deli cartons to freeze.

To serve, heat in pan and serve on toast or add cream cheese or mayonnaise for paté.

William Miller
Fond du Lac, Wisconsin

BUFFALO JERKY

1½ to 2 lbs. buffalo meat
1-oz. pkg. instant meat marinade
¼ tsp. garlic powder
¼ tsp. onion powder
¼ tsp. black pepper
½ tsp. Tabasco sauce
1¾ cups cold water
½ tsp. liquid smoke

Cut meat with the grain into 6-inch strips about 1½-inches wide and ½ inch thick. Set aside. In large glass bowl, combine instant meat marinade, garlic powder, onion powder, black pepper, Tabasco sauce, cold water and liquid smoke; mix well. Pierce meat deeply with fork and place in marinade; mix well to coat. Cover and refrigerate overnight. Remove meat from marinade and drain slightly. Place on rack, making sure strips do not overlap. Place baking sheet under rack and dry for 5 hours at 150°F to 175°F. Cool and store in covered container in refrigerator. These larger pieces are not dried long and will be soft.

Tim Krueger
Oshkosh, Wisconsin

Venison Salami

7 to 8 lbs. venison or elk
2 to 3 lbs. pork fat
1 pt. ice water
6 T. non-iodized salt
2 tsp. Prague Powder #1
2 cups soy flour
1 T. white pepper
2 T. nutmeg
2 large cloves garlic
6 T. corn syrup solids
2 T. light corn syrup

Grind meat and fat through large plate on grinder. Mix water, salt, Prague Powder, flour, pepper, nutmeg, garlic, corn syrup solids and corn syrup; stir well. Blend with meat mixture. Place in cooler for 24 hours. Remove from cooler and regrind through smallest plate possible. After grinding, add water to mixture if necessary to make stuffing casings easier.

Stuff salami into largest casing available, being sure to pick all air pockets out of casings by ice pick, fork or other sharp instrument.

Place in smoker with vent wide open at 120°F to 130°F for about 1 hour. Raise temperature to 150°F and smoke for approximately 1 hour. Raise temperature to 165°F and hold until internal temperature of sausage reaches 152°F. Shower with cold water until internal temperature is approximately 120°F. Cool overnight before slicing.

Note: Variations in amount of meat vs. fat allow for individual taste in salami; try a leaner mixture and then increase fat, if desired.

Ernest Terry
Wichita Falls, Texas

Ring Bologna

15 lbs. venison, cut into chunks
   and ground
2 T. seasoned meat cure
2 tsp. red pepper flakes
1 T. garlic powder
6 T. salt
1½ tsp. whole mustard seed
2 tsp. black pepper

Add meat cure, red pepper flakes, garlic powder, salt, mustard seed and black pepper; if meat is dry, add up to 2 cups water. Grind meat again. Stuff meat into beef or pig casings in 24-inch lengths and tie together. Allow to hang for 1 hour before placing in smokehouse. Smoke for 10 hours; cook at 170°F for 30 minutes. Store in freezer; cook as desired before serving.

Jerry Himes
Milroy, Pennsylvania

Fresh Polish Sausage

10 lbs. game meat, coarsely ground
4 T. salt
2 T. pepper
1 T. coriander
1 T. paprika
1 T. allspice
1 tsp. marjoram
2 cups ice water

Combine meat with salt, pepper, coriander, paprika, allspice and marjoram. Add water and mix thoroughly using your hands to knead mixture. Fill casings loosely, leaving 1 inch at each end. Tie off ends. Refrigerate to use within 5 days or freeze up to 2 months.

Kevin Kilmartin
Philadelphia, Pennsylvania

GREAT WHITE HUNTER JERKY

Meat of choice
2 cups Worcestershire sauce
2 cups teriyaki marinade
2 cups soy sauce
1 cup lemon juice
4 T. seasoned salt
16 drops liquid smoke
4 T. garlic salt
2 T. onion powder or onion salt
2 tsp. pepper
½ oz. Tabasco sauce
½ to 1 cup maple syrup

Cut meat into ¼-inch strips. Mix Worcestershire sauce, teriyaki marinade, soy sauce, lemon juice, seasoned salt, liquid smoke, garlic salt, onion powder or salt, pepper, Tabasco sauce and maple syrup. Layer strips in glass dish, alternating a layer of meat then covering it with marinade, and so on. When dish is full, cover with plastic wrap; do not use foil. Refrigerate for at least 24 hours. Remove meat from marinade and place in dehydrator until dry enough for your taste. Can also be place in 200°F oven with door slightly open. Vacuum seal in small bags and store until you need a treat or go hiking or hunting.

Note: Can be used for venison, caribou, duck, goose

Clair A. Glantz
Pueblo, Colorado

TROUTS' DEER JERKY

5 to 7 lbs. thinly sliced deer meat
 cut into strips; back ham meat
 works best
¼ cup Worcestershire sauce
¼ cup soy sauce
¼ cup teriyaki sauce
4 to 6 oz. steak sauce
2 tsp. lemon juice
3 to 6 oz. liquid smoke
1 T. garlic pepper
1 T. onion powder
1 T. Caribbean Jerk Seasoning
 (Sweet & Spicy)
Tabasco sauce or crushed red
 pepper (optional)

In large bowl, combine Worcestershire sauce, soy sauce, teriyaki sauce, steak sauce, lemon juice, liquid smoke, garlic pepper, onion powder, jerk seasoning and Tabasco sauce. Add meat and stir well to coat all pieces thoroughly. Cover and refrigerate for 18 to 24 hours, turning a couple of times. After soaking, place meat strips on dehydrator trays sprayed with cooking spray or on baking sheets lined with aluminum foil. (Hint: Make ridges with foil to help moisture drain away from meat.)

If using dehydrator, cook for 4 to 6 hours, checking every couple of hours; turning meat is optional. For oven drying, place baking sheets in preheated 180°F oven for 4 to 6 hours, turning meat a couple of times.

For best results, meat should be sliced ⅛ to ¼ inch thick. Jerky can be refrigerated when done to keep longer.

William Trout Jr.
Bridgeton, New Jersey

BACON-WRAPPED JERKY

Steak or roast, 1- to 1½-inch-thick slices
Bacon
½ cup soy sauce
½ cup Worcestershire sauce
½ cup liquid smoke
Dash of Tabasco sauce

Wrap meat with bacon and secure with toothpicks. Mix soy sauce, Worcestershire sauce, liquid smoke and Tabasco sauce. Add wrapped meat slices and marinate for 2 to 4 hours. Cook in broiler or on grill, turning halfway through cooking time.

Elbert Salsman
Amarillo, Texas

Rusty's 12-Gauge Pheasant Sausage

28 oz. uncooked pheasant, turkey or
    goose meat (legs, thighs and/or breast)
4 oz. pork fat
2 T. ice cold water
2¾ tsp. salt
1⅛ tsp. finely ground black pepper
¾ tsp. cayenne pepper
½ tsp. coriander
⅛ tsp. nutmeg
3¾ tsp. sugar
5 oz. coarsely shredded cheddar cheese,
    slightly frozen
1½ oz. minced chili peppers (jalapeño)
Oil

Slightly freeze pheasant and debone; remove bloodshot areas and all shot. Grind meat through largest plate of grinder or mince meat by hand with a sharp knife. Grind pork fat through medium or fine plate of grinder. Mix meat and fat with water and salt. Mix in black pepper, cayenne pepper, coriander, nutmeg, sugar, cheese and chili peppers. Stuff into hog casings. Link sausages to about 4 inches in length. Tie off ends of each sausage. Cook in skillet with oil until done (internal temperature of 152°F). Can be frozen. Serve with wild rice, noodles with garlic butter and asparagus tips.

Smoked alternative: Omit sugar, increase water to a total of 1 cup and add ⅜ tsp. cure salt. Smoke in preheated smoker at 135°F with no smoke. After 1 hour, increase temperature to 160°F with hickory or apple wood smoke until internal temperature is 152°F. When done, shower (wash) in cold water (in sink) until internal temperature drops below 115°F. Refrigerate or freeze.

Tip: *Keep sausage mixture cold (between 34°F and 40°F) for best grinding results.*

Russell Tait
Laramie, Wyoming

Smoked Bear

1 bear hind quarter, boned and trimmed
Salt
Cayenne pepper

Sprinkle hind quarter with salt and cayenne pepper. Place in smoker with water pan and fruitwood or other hardwood until meat is well done. Refrigerate until meat is cold. Thinly slice across grain and use for lunch meat.

O. J. Utton
Chama, New Mexico

Teriyaki Rice Vinegar Jerky

5 lbs. ground venison
1 cup teriyaki sauce
2 cups soy sauce
4 oz. liquid smoke
2 tsp. seasoned rice vinegar
1 T. onion powder
1 tsp. garlic powder
5 T. packed brown sugar
Pepper

Mix teriyaki sauce, soy sauce, liquid smoke, rice vinegar, onion powder, garlic powder and brown sugar. Mix with ground venison. Marinate for 1 hour; drain in colander. Put through jerky gun and place on trays in dehydrator. Season with pepper. Dry until flexible or the way you prefer. This recipe can be prepared the traditional way also.

Howell Parrent
Taft, California

Chorizo (Mexican Breakfast Sausage)

CHORIZO
(MEXICAN BREAKFAST SAUSAGE)

1 lb. ground venison
1 lb. ground pork
1 clove garlic, crushed
½ cup ground red pepper
1 tsp. black pepper
¼ tsp. cloves
¼ tsp. cinnamon
¼ tsp. oregano
¼ cup cumin
½ tsp. salt
1 T. oregano leaves
½ cup vinegar
2 T. water
10 small hot dried red chiles (chile el monte, tepine chile or Thai dragon chile)

Mix venison and pork; set aside. Combine garlic, ground red pepper, black pepper, cloves, cinnamon, oregano, cumin, salt, oregano leaves, vinegar, water and dried red chiles in blender; purée. Knead into meat mixture until thoroughly blended. Cover and refrigerate for 24 hours. Divide into ¼- to ½-pound portions and freeze. To use, crumble and fry, then combine with eggs, refried beans or diced potatoes. Cover with picante sauce and wrap in flour tortilla; serve as breakfast tacos.

Robert Solis
Edinburg, Texas

Jamaican Smoked Chicken, Partridge, Pheasant or Dove

3 lbs. bird of choice, split
½ cup chili sauce
½ tsp. basil
½ tsp. dill weed
2 T. cider vinegar
1 tsp. salt
½ tsp. pepper
1 T. Worcestershire sauce
½ tsp. dry mustard
½ cup minced onion
2 cloves garlic, minced
2 T. vegetable oil

Fill water pan ¾ full of water. Rinse meat and pat dry. Combine chili sauce, basil, dill weed, cider vinegar, salt, pepper, Worcestershire sauce, dry mustard, onion, garlic and oil in a bowl. Reserve some liquid to use later as serving sauce. Place meat in a plastic bowl. Pour marinade over meat and refrigerate for 4 to 6 hours. Remove meat from marinade and place on grill. Brush some marinade over meat before covering smoker. Discard remaining marinade. Heat reserved liquid and serve along with meat.

Rob Wodzinski
Iron River, Michigan

Mild Venison Gumbo

1 lb. venison bratwurst
1 lb. venison Cajun sausage
1 lb. Italian pork sausage
1 lb. medium shrimp, cooked
32-oz. can diced tomatoes
16-oz. can tomato sauce
1½ cups carrots, sliced
1½ cups celery, sliced
4 cups water
1 T. black pepper
1 T. salt
½ tsp. thyme
½ tsp. oregano
2 bay leaves
½ cup olive oil
¼ cup chopped garlic
1 bunch green onions, sliced
1 yellow onion, chopped
1 green pepper, chopped
1 red pepper, chopped
1 lb. frozen okra, cut

Brown bratwurst, Cajun sausage and Italian sausage in large frying pan. Drain in colander and dry with paper towels. In large pot, combine tomatoes, tomato sauce, carrots, celery, water and spices; cook over medium heat. Heat olive oil in medium frying pan. Add garlic, onions and peppers; sauté until tender. When done, add to pot and increase temperature. Add sausage, shrimp and okra; bring to a boil for approximately 10 minutes. Reduce heat to low and simmer until ready to eat. Serve over rice or noodles, if desired. Accompany with French bread and butter for dipping.

Note: For a hotter version, add 2 tablespoons hot sauce or ¼ tablespoon cayenne pepper.

Rob Lombardo
Plainfield, Illinois

SMOKED DUCK OR GOOSE

18 duck breast filets or 12 goose breast filets or
  a combination that will fit into your smoker
1 tub brining solution (see below)
Your favorite dried spices (i.e. onion powder,
  etc.)
Hickory or mesquite wood chips

BRINING SOLUTION FOR COOL SMOKING

4 qts. water
2 cups pickling or kosher salt
2 cups granulated sugar
1 large onion, coarsely chopped
2 to 3 bay leaves
6 to 8 whole cloves
6 cloves garlic, crushed

Brine the filets for 4 to 6 hours. Rinse under cool running water, pat dry with paper towels and put on drying racks. Add dried spices if your brine was unseasoned. Dry for 1 to 1½ hours. Smoke for 6 to 8 hours, following smoker directions. Once meat begins to shrink and feel well-done, remove to baking sheets and put in oven for 5 to 10 minutes or until meat just begins to sizzle. Cool and pack in airtight container. Place in refrigerator overnight for fullest flavor. Keeps 6 months if wrapped tightly in plastic wrap and frozen. Thinly sliced, the center of each filet will be pink and moist. Serve with crackers and horseradish.

This is a basic brining solution to be used when preparing meats and fish for slow smoking. You can delete all of the spices and aromatic vegetables if you would rather work with powdered spices later on in the process. I have used both methods extensively and find that they work about the same. I just use whatever I happen to have in the pantry.

Combine water, salt, sugar, onion, bay leaves, cloves and garlic in a 2½ gallon pot. Bring almost to a boil, stirring steadily with spoon or whisk until all sugar and salt are completely dissolved. Remove from stove and cool to room temperature.

Note: Honey may be substituted for sugar; decrease salt if using soy sauce or Worcestershire sauce.

Jim Sklarz
Holden, Massachusetts

SMOKED WILD BOAR

1 small to medium wild boar roast
¾ T. salt
1 tsp. onion powder
1 tsp. garlic powder
1 tsp. Accent (optional)
½ tsp. pepper
⅓ cup Worcestershire sauce
¼ cup soy sauce
1 tsp. liquid smoke

SAUCE

2 T. Worcestershire sauce
1 T. garlic powder
1 tsp. onion powder
1 bottle sweet barbecue sauce

Mix salt, onion powder, garlic powder, Accent, pepper, Worcestershire sauce, soy sauce and liquid smoke in large glass bowl. Add meat, cover and refrigerate for 24 hours. Remove from marinade and smoke for 24 hours.

After 24 hours, remove meat from smoker and debone.

Combine Worcestershire sauce, garlic powder, onion powder and barbecue sauce in large bowl. Add meat and mix well. Mash meat into little pieces with fork. Great for sandwiches or with a main meal.

Gerald Livingston
Seymour, Texas

Venison Breakfast Sausage

40 lbs. venison
20 lbs. pork
½ cup curing salt
¼ cup packed brown sugar
2 oz. black pepper
1 pkg. Old Plantation Seasoning
1 cup ground onion
½ T. allspice
½ T. ginger
¼ T. nutmeg

Grind venison and pork together; mix with salt, brown sugar, pepper, seasoning, onion, allspice, ginger and nutmeg. Sprinkle with water while mixing together until sticky. Package in 1-pound packages or use casings to stuff to desired size.

Larry Freese
Brooten, Minnesota

Venison Jerky with Whiskey

7 lbs. venison
3½ cups white sugar
4½ tsp. fresh grated garlic
2½ tsp. fresh grated gingerroot
1½ tsp. cayenne powder
2 tsp. dried red pepper
1 tsp. coarse black pepper
4 cups low-sodium soy sauce
⅓ cup whiskey
5 T. roasted sesame seeds
1½ cups finely chopped green onion
2 tsp. sesame oil

Slice venison to ¼-inch thickness. Rinse venison and squeeze all excess blood and water out. (This step is very important for marinade to soak into venison.) In large bowl, mash sugar, garlic, ginger, cayenne powder, red pepper and black pepper with back of tablespoon. This will draw out all juices from garlic and gingerroot. Add soy sauce and whiskey. Place venison in large pan and use hands to work marinade into venison. Add sesame seeds and green onion. Cover and refrigerate for 2 days.

Two hours before smoking, mix sesame oil into marinated venison and let sit. After 2 hours, hang each piece on a stainless steel hook and hang on smoke sticks. Make sure the pieces are not touching.

Preheat smokehouse to 150°F; hang jerky in smokehouse and keep temperature at 150°F for first hour. For next 2 hours, keep temperature at 200°F. Remove from smokehouse, take hooks off and let cool completely. Cut into 1-inch strips; bag and freeze.

Sidney and Berna Feuella
Makawao, Maui, Hawaii

Alaskan Quick Jerky

2 lbs. ground elk or venison
⅓ cup soy sauce
⅓ cup red wine
2 T. Worcestershire sauce
½ tsp. pepper
½ tsp. onion powder
½ tsp. garlic powder
¼ tsp. ginger
⅛ tsp. nutmeg
2 tsp. cayenne pepper flakes (optional amount)

Mix soy sauce, wine, Worcestershire sauce, pepper, onion powder, garlic powder, ginger, nutmeg and cayenne pepper flakes; mix well. Add to meat and knead thoroughly.

Line baking sheet with waxed paper. Spread half of meat mixture thinly across entire baking sheet using rolling pin, bottle or hands. When spread to uniform thickness of ⅛ to ¼ inch, invert onto standard cookie cooling rack and remove waxed paper. Repeat with other half of mixture. Bake for 4 to 6 hours at 170°F to 190°F or until as crisp as desired. Halfway through cooking time, excess fat can be blotted off with a paper towel if required. Remove from oven, allow to cool and cut into strips with standard, clean scissors. Store in cool place or refrigerator.

David Flagg
Albuquerque, New Mexico

Smoked Goose Jerky

6 goose breasts
12-oz. bottle Lawry's Mesquite Marinade
1⅛ cups Worcestershire sauce
3 T. Louisiana hot sauce
2 T. liquid smoke
2 T. black pepper
2 T. garlic salt
6 (12-oz.) cans beer

Cut partially frozen goose breasts ¼ inch thick. Mix Mesquite Marinade, Worcestershire sauce, Louisiana hot sauce, liquid smoke, black pepper and garlic salt. Add meat and refrigerate for 24 hours. Fill bottom pan with charcoal and let it get gray. Fill water pan with beer and top off with water. Place jerky strips on racks and smoke for 3 hours. Do not overcook.

Recipe can be used for venison or other wild game.

Brian Gross
Oakley, Michigan

Venison Sausage Cheeseballs

2 lbs. venison sausage
1½ cups all-purpose baking/biscuit mix
4 cups shredded sharp cheddar cheese
½ cup finely chopped onion
½ cup finely chopped celery
½ tsp. garlic powder

Mix sausage, baking mix, cheese, onion, celery and garlic powder. Shape into 1-inch balls and place on ungreased baking sheet. Bake for 15 minutes at 375°F or until golden brown. Makes about 6 dozen cheese balls. Can be frozen uncooked.

Bob Pozner
Minnetonka, Minnesota

SMOKED WILD DUCK

1 large or 2 to 3 small ducks, skin left on
½ tsp. onion powder
½ tsp. celery salt
1 tsp. black pepper
⅓ cup non-iodized salt
½ tsp. dill weed
1 T. packed brown sugar
1 tsp. dry mustard
1 empty beer or soda can per duck
Apple cider or beer

Combine onion powder, celery salt, pepper, non-iodized salt, dill weed, brown sugar, dry mustard. Rub mixture on skin and into cavity. Refrigerate overnight to absorb cure. The next day, remove from refrigerator and rinse cure off skin prior to smoking. Start smoker, using 50/50 mix of alder and hickory.

Fill beer can ¼ to ½ full with apple cider or beer. Insert a can into cavity of each bird. Stand in smoker. Smoke in heavy smoke for 8 to 9 hours at 125°F. When done, discard can and contents, enjoy smoked duck with cheese and crackers or on baguette slices with mustard and herbs.

Mike Gandolfo
Coeur d'Alene, Idaho

OLD COUNTRY (YUGOSLAVIA) SAUSAGE

10 lbs. diced game meat
10 lbs. diced fatty pork shoulder
Heaping ⅓ cup salt
3 T. plus 1 tsp. sage
10 cloves garlic, crushed
8 tsp. onion powder
7 tsp. black pepper
5 tsp. whole mustard seed

Mix game meat and pork. Add salt, sage, garlic, onion powder, black pepper and mustard seed. Grind through a ⅜-inch plate and stuff into hog casings in bratwurst-size links. May be packaged and frozen. Boil until fully cooked and serve. May be cooked on grill.

Steve Greiner
Loveland, Colorado

MUSTARD ELK JERKY

2 lbs. elk or venison, cut with grain into ½-inch strips
1 T. salt
1 tsp. onion powder
1 tsp. garlic powder
1 to 2 tsp. pepper
⅓ cup Worcestershire sauce
¼ cup soy sauce
1 T. Grey Poupon or stone ground mustard

Place meat in glass container. Combine salt, onion powder, garlic powder, pepper, Worcestershire sauce, soy sauce and mustard; mix with whisk. Pour over meat and marinate overnight. Put in dehydrator or oven until dry. Strips will be more chewy and easier to eat.

Babe Love
Loveland, Colorado

Smoked Wild Duck

Venison Breakfast Sausage

1 lb. venison
½ lb. pork shoulder
¾ tsp. salt
1 tsp. dried sage leaves
½ tsp. ground gingerroot
½ tsp. pepper
1 T. molasses

Cut venison and pork into ¾-inch cubes. Mix salt, sage, gingerroot and pepper in a bowl. Cover meat completely. Add molasses. Cover and refrigerate overnight. Mix by hand to ensure a good covering of marinade. Grind meat and form patties; fry in skillet.

Rob Kopp
Huber Heights, Ohio

Elmer Fudd's Sausage

3 lbs. ground venison
1 lb. ground pork
3 T. liquid smoke
2 T. Worcestershire sauce
1 T. soy sauce
2 T. coarsely ground pepper
1½ T. Colman's English mustard blend
1 T. Szechuan pepper blend
1 T. garlic powder
1½ tsp. crushed red pepper

Blend venison and pork. Mix liquid smoke, Worcestershire sauce, soy sauce, pepper, mustard blend, pepper blend, garlic powder and red pepper. Blend with meat in glass bowl. Cover and refrigerate for 3 days. Mix well on the third day, then form 8 (6-inch) logs, 1½ inches in diameter, on plastic wrap. Wrap in plastic wrap as tightly as possible. Refrigerate for 3 more days. Unwrap on third day and place on broiler rack to drain any grease and bake for 1½ hours at 275°F. Remove and let cool.

Michael Pitts
Gardner, Kansas

Jerky Marinade
with Chokecherry Wine

5 lbs. lean meat, thinly sliced
¼ cup salt
2 T. coarse black pepper
2 cups chokecherry wine (any red wine will do)
1 T. liquid smoke
1 medium onion, finely chopped
2 tsp. cloves
1½ tsp. garlic powder
½ tsp. dry mustard
½ tsp. dill weed
½ tsp. basil leaves
1 T. soy sauce
3 T. Cajun seasoning
1 cup cold water

In large bowl, combine salt, pepper, wine, liquid smoke, onion, cloves, garlic powder, dry mustard, dill weed, basil leaves, soy sauce, Cajun seasoning and water. Mix thoroughly. Add meat strips, making sure meat is completely submerged. You can use a heavy plate to keep it submerged. Refrigerate for 24 to 48 hours before placing in dehydrator.

Rob Wodzinski
Iron River, Michigan

ALFRED'S ORIENTAL VENISON JERKY

4 lbs. venison roast
2 oz. brandy or bourbon
¼ cup salt
½ tsp. onion powder
½ tsp. garlic powder
1 tsp. ginger
¼ cup packed brown sugar
1 cup apple cider or cider vinegar
1 tsp. orange peel, grated
½ cup soy sauce
2 cups water
6 white cloves (optional)

Trim fat from meat and cut into ¼- to ½-inch slices. In large glass bowl, mix brandy or bourbon, salt, onion powder, garlic powder, ginger, brown sugar, cider or vinegar, orange peel, soy sauce, water and cloves. Add meat and refrigerate for 8 hours. Remove from marinade. Place on rack and allow to air dry until glazed. Do not rinse. Smoke for 12 to 16 hours, depending on degree of dryness you prefer. Use 3 pans full of hickory or cherry wood chips to add special flavor to meat.

Tim Krueger
Oshkosh, Wisconsin

SMOKED ELK ROAST

6- to 8-lb. elk rump roast
6 cloves garlic, sliced
1 rib celery
6 slices of bacon
Salt
Pepper
Sweet paprika
Worcestershire sauce
Olive oil
Red wine
Water
1 onion, sliced
Parsley flakes
½ lemon

Put slits in roast with knife. In each slit put a large slice of garlic, celery and bacon. Mix salt, pepper, paprika and Worcestershire sauce in a small bowl. Rub over roast. Brown roast in olive oil in large skillet. Have water pan smoker ready by this time, using hickory and mesquite chunks. Put red wine and water in pan, saving a little wine. Put roast in smoker on top rack on a piece of foil. Pour olive oil from skillet and remaining wine over roast. Season roast again with salt and pepper and any other seasonings you prefer. Put 3 slices of bacon and 3 or 4 slices of onion on top of roast, using toothpicks to hold in place. Sprinkle with parsley flakes and paprika. Smoke to desired doneness or for at least 4 hours. Squeeze half of lemon over roast when done. Serve with scalloped potatoes and sweet corn.

Dave Kulaszewski
Cleveland, Ohio

SANDHILL CRANE JERKY

Breast of sandhill crane, sliced
    ¼ inch thick
Soy sauce
Liquid smoke
Fresh crushed garlic
Black pepper

Place meat slices in glass baking dish. Create mixture of ⅔ soy sauce to ⅓ liquid smoke. Add garlic and black pepper; pour over meat. Marinate overnight. Remove meat from marinade and drain on paper towels.

For a water smoker, use 10 pounds hardwood charcoal. When coals are gray, add hickory chips that were soaked overnight. Fill water pan. Put meat on smoker racks. Smoke for 6 to 8 hours, adding hickory chips and coals as needed. Meat is done when it is dry and will bend but not break.

Randy Jacobs
Lubbock, Texas

Smoked Venison Meatloaf

2 lbs. ground venison
½ lb. ground pork sausage
1 cup bread crumbs
1 cup oats
1 cup diced onion
½ cup diced green bell pepper
½ cup cubed cheddar cheese
½ cup ketchup
½ tsp. garlic powder
1 T. parsley
1 egg, lightly beaten
Salt
Pepper
1 tsp. Worcestershire sauce
¼ cup honey
3 slices bacon

Mix venison and pork. Add bread crumbs, oats, diced onion, green bell pepper, cheese, ketchup, garlic powder, parsley, egg, salt, pepper, Worcestershire sauce and honey; mix well. Form loaf and place in loaf pan. Top with bacon. Drizzle additional honey on top. Put in smoker until done, using meat thermometer for doneness. Can use apple or hickory or your favorite smoking wood.

Steven R. Hall
Williamsport, Pennsylvania

Sweet Kickin' Jerky

1 lb. elk or venison, well trimmed
   (elk works best)
2 T. salt
2 T. spicy seasoned salt
1 T. pepper
2 T. cayenne pepper
2 T. onion powder
1 T. garlic powder
2 T. dry mustard
1 T. chopped garlic
2 T. minced onion
6 T. packed brown sugar
1 cup Worcestershire sauce
1 cup hot ketchup

Combine salt, seasoned salt, pepper, cayenne pepper, onion powder, garlic powder, dry mustard, chopped garlic, minced onion, brown sugar, Worcestershire sauce and ketchup. Mix well with hand mixer on high speed. Pour enough of mixture into glass pan to cover bottom. Layer marinade and meat until you run out of meat. Refrigerate for 24 hours, turning or stirring meat at least 6 times. Spray dehydrator trays with cooking spray before putting meat on them; it makes removing the meat and cleanup a lot easier. Place meat on racks, being careful not to overlap pieces. Dry to your preference; the longer you dry it, the more brittle and the harder it gets. Dry for at least 12 hours. I dry it for 18 hours; it is still soft but not too chewy.

Randy Larrison
Santa Maria, California

Duck or Goose Jerky

6 goose breast filets or 8 to 9 duck
   breast filets
2 qts. brining solution

Cut filets lengthwise into ¼-inch strips. Brine for 3 to 4 hours. Rinse and pat dry, then put on drying racks for about 1 hour. Spread pieces on smoker racks and place in smoker. Burn 3 pans of chips. Jerky is done when meat shrivels and dries. Pack in airtight container in refrigerator overnight before using.

Jim Sklarz
Holden, Massachusetts

Smoked Venison Meatloaf

HEADCHEESE WITHOUT THE HEAD

4 deer shanks or 2 moose shanks
4 pork hocks
Salt
Pepper
Garlic salt
2 large onions, chopped
Onion salt

Cut meat from bones, then into very small pieces. Put meat and bones into a large pot. Cover with water. Add salt, pepper, garlic salt, onions and onion salt. Cover and boil slowly until well-done; meat will fall from bones. When done, remove bones and pour into loaf pans. Cool well. When set, slice for sandwiches.

Susan Leroux
Peers, Alberta, Canada

BRINE-CURED JERKY

Sweet Brine Cure
3 gal. water
5½ lbs. salt
3½ cups packedbrown sugar
6 crushed bay leaves
3 T. black pepper

Mix water, salt, brown sugar, bay leaves and black pepper. Cut lean meat into long, wide slabs about 1 inch thick; add to brine and mix well. Cure for 3 to 6 days. Rinse and dry in cool place. Use a sharp knife to slice meat lengthwise into ¼-inch-wide slices (easiest to cut if meat is near freezing point). Hang slices on racks and cold smoke at 75ºF to 85ºF for 12 to 36 hours. If jerky snaps rather than folds when bent, it is ready.

Judy Gauthier
Athabasca, Alberta, Canada

DUSTIN'S SUMMER SAUSAGE

3 lbs. ground venison or other wild
   game
2½ level T. curing salt
1½ cups water
3 tsp. liquid smoke
½ tsp. white pepper
½ tsp. whole mustard seed
½ tsp. dry mustard
½ tsp. sweet pepper flakes
1 tsp. dried sage
¾ tsp. onion powder or onion flakes or
   ½ cup finely chopped onion
1 tsp. garlic powder or 1 clove garlic,
   finely minced

Mix meat with curing salt, water, liquid smoke, white pepper, whole mustard seed, dry mustard, sweet pepper flakes, dried sage, onion powder and garlic powder. Store, covered, in refrigerator overnight. Form into patties and separate with waxed paper. Seal enough for a meal in freezer bags and freeze until ready to use.

To use: Thaw completely and fry like hamburgers.

Variation: Mix as above. Shape into 3 (2½-inch) loaves; wrap tightly in aluminum foil; store in refrigerator overnight. Puncture all over bottom of each loaf with a fork. Place on wire rack over shallow baking dish and bake at 325ºF for 1 hour 45 minutes. Eat immediately or cool and refrigerate until ready to use. Can also be cased and smoked.

Dustin J. Hill
Goodman, Missouri

SMOKED DOVE BREASTS

**40 to 50 dove breasts,
washed
Olive oil
Lemon pepper
1 onion, sliced
4 oz. butter
Salt
Black pepper**

Make foil pan 2 or 3 layers thick, large enough to hold all dove breasts with a 3- to 4-inch overlap around all edges. Place breasts bone-side down and fold up edges to form a leakproof pan. Pour a small amount of olive oil over breasts. Sprinkle generously with lemon pepper. Place onion slices on top of doves. Cut butter in half and place on top. Cook over wood fire with plenty of smoke for 1½ hours at 250°F to 300°F. When done, serve hot in juices. Season with salt and pepper.

Jimmy Lee McKnight
Lorena, Texas

MANDARIN SMOKED QUAIL

**12 quail (or other wild fowl)
2 (15-oz.) cans mandarin oranges, reserve juice
1 bottle of your favorite white wine
9-oz. box raisins
½-pt. bottle of your favorite brandy
1-lb. pkg. wild rice
¾ cup butter, divided
Garlic salt
Freshly ground pepper
Lemon pepper
1-lb. pkg. thick-sliced hickory smoked bacon**

Marinate the quail in juice from mandarin oranges mixed with white wine for a minimum of 2 to 3 hours. Remove quail; save marinade. Marinate oranges and raisins in brandy for 1 to 2 hours. Remove from brandy and strain; save marinade. Cook wild rice until done; stir in strained oranges and raisins.

Use rice mixture to stuff cavity of each bird, then add 1 tablespoon butter. Season outside of each bird to your taste with garlic salt, freshly ground pepper and lemon pepper. Wrap each bird with bacon; this also helps hold stuffing in. Use toothpicks if needed to hold bacon in place.

Once you have a full pan of hot coals in your smoker, pour the leftover marinades into the fluid pan. Place quail on top rack and put smoker lid on. Smoke birds for 5 to 6 hours on medium setting. Add your favorite flavor of wood chips (apple, hickory or mesquite are my favorites) throughout cooking time.

Note:
- *Continue adding water to keep fluid pan FULL throughout cooking; this will help keep your bird moist.*
- *Soak wood chips in water the night before to get more smoke and flavor.*
- *Add dry chunks of wood to keep a good bed of coals going.*
- *Try to smoke on medium temperature for longer periods of time for the most tender, full-flavored, juicy bird you have ever tasted!*

Jeff Tschetter
Phoenix, Arizona

Spicy Duck Sausage

Spicy Duck Sausage

2 deboned ducks, diced
½ lb. bacon
3 T. fresh minced garlic
3 T. minced shallots
3 T. chopped parsley
½ cup chopped fresh basil
1 tsp. oregano
1 tsp. dried basil
1 tsp. thyme
1 tsp. salt
1 tsp. black pepper
½ tsp. white pepper
¼ tsp. cayenne pepper
1 tsp. mustard powder
1 tsp. onion powder
1 tsp. granulated garlic
Sausage casings

Mix duck, bacon, garlic, shallots, parsley, fresh basil, oregano, dried basil, thyme, salt, black pepper, white pepper, cayenne pepper, mustard powder, onion powder and garlic in a large bowl. Cover and place in freezer for 20 minutes (partially frozen meat grinds better). Run through meat grinder and stuff into casings. Tie off into 4- to 5-inch lengths with butcher's twine. Poke sausages with a meat fork to allow air to escape.

Cooking Option 1: Soak sausages overnight in beer. Grill and serve with favorite zesty mustard.

Cooking Option 2: Smoke sausage. Place sausage in smoker and cook for 10 to 15 minutes.

George Transue Jr.
Bates City, Missouri

Smoked Duck or Goose Spread

8 smoked duck filets or 4 smoked
  goose filets
2 (8-oz.) pkgs. cream cheese
2 tsp. minced garlic
6 to 8 dashes Louisiana hot sauce
2 T. fresh lemon juice

Good for smoked meats that come out too dry or too salty. Coarsely chop filets. Put in food processor and pulse until filets are pulverized. Add cream cheese, garlic, hot sauce and lemon juice. Blend until smooth. Pack into plastic wrap-lined bowl or decorative mold. Chill for 2 hours. Invert mold or bowl on decorative plate, gently tap surface to release spread; remove plastic wrap. Garnish with herbs and serve with crackers, toast points or bread sticks.

Jim Sklarz
Holden, Massachusetts

Venison Breakfast Sausage

3 lbs. ground venison
2 lbs. ground lean pork
4 T. Morton Tender Quick
2 tsp. dry mustard
½ tsp. white pepper
2 tsp. onion powder
2 tsp. garlic powder
4 tsp. liquid smoke
½ tsp. rubbed sage
1½ tsp. poultry seasoning
1½ tsp. cayenne pepper
2 cups water

Mix venison and pork. Combine Tender Quick, dry mustard, white pepper, onion powder, garlic powder, liquid smoke, sage, poultry seasoning, cayenne pepper and water. Blend mixture with meat mixture. Form into patties and freeze until needed.

Colleen Point
Hibbing, Minnesota
Submitted by son Jon Point
Deer River, Minnesota

Soft Jerky

2 lbs. moose, elk or venison
1 T. peanut oil or other cooking oil
⅓ cup soy sauce
½ tsp. garlic salt
2 cloves garlic, thinly sliced and diced
½ tsp. ground black pepper
4 to 6 green onions, thinly sliced and
  diced
Salt
Pepper

Trim all fat from meat and cut into 1- to 2-inch-thick pieces; thinly slice into strips. Set aside. Mix oil, soy sauce, garlic salt, garlic, pepper and onion. Pour over meat and toss to coat thoroughly. Cover and refrigerate for 2 to 8 hours or up to 24 hours, stirring occasionally. Cook on medium high in large frying pan or in wok, stirring frequently. Cook about ¼ of meat at a time. Salt and pepper to taste. Store in zip-top bags in refrigerator or freezer. Great for snacking. If desired, enclose in foil and put on grill to take chill out.

Kenneth D. Holt
Buhl, Idaho

DEER BOLOGNA

5 lbs. ground deer meat
5 tsp. quick cure
2 tsp. whole mustard seed
½ tsp. dry ground mustard
1 tsp. hickory smoke salt
2 tsp. crushed red pepper (optional)
1 tsp. coarsely ground black pepper
1 tsp. Accent
2½ tsp. garlic salt
1 tsp. garlic powder
4 T. packed brown sugar
4 T. honey or pancake syrup

In large bowl, combine quick cure, mustard seed, ground mustard, hickory smoke salt, red pepper, black pepper, Accent, garlic salt, garlic powder, brown sugar and honey or pancake syrup; mix well with meat. Shape into 2 or 3 rolls and wrap in wax paper. Refrigerate for 3 days. Remove paper and bake on wire rack with drip pan underneath for 1 hour at 350°F. Turn rolls and bake for an additional 30 minutes.

Edward Sibole
Gerrardstown, West Virginia

SMOKED WILD TURKEY

1 wild turkey
2 apples, thinly sliced
8 slices bacon
½ qt. apple juice in spray bottle

Carefully separate skin from turkey and place apple slices between skin and meat. Secure apple slices to outside of skin with toothpicks. Wrap bacon around turkey; especially cover breast and legs. Wrap entire bird in cheesecloth. Soak cheesecloth with apple juice, using spray bottle. Smoke turkey at 225°F until inner temperature is 185°F. Occasionally spray cheesecloth with apple juice.

Stephen Gingras
Lowell, Massachusetts

FAITH'S 5-ALARM PERKY JERKY

5 lbs. venison
1 tsp. Old Bay seasoning
1 tsp. red pepper
1 tsp. cayenne pepper
1 tsp. chili powder
1 tsp. onion powder
1 tsp. garlic powder
½ tsp. dry mustard
½ cup soy sauce
½ cup Worcestershire sauce
1 cup water or beer (optional)
1 onion, minced

Mix Old Bay, red pepper, cayenne pepper, chili powder, onion powder, garlic powder, dry mustard, soy sauce, Worcestershire sauce, water or beer and onion in glass bowl. Slice venison into thin slices and add to mixture in bowl; mix well. Marinate for 24 hours. Place on toothpicks and put on highest rack in oven for 8 to 10 hours at 150°F. Let cool for about 10 minutes.

Faith Novak
Edgewood, Maryland

INDEX